discovering science

Open ersity

Energy

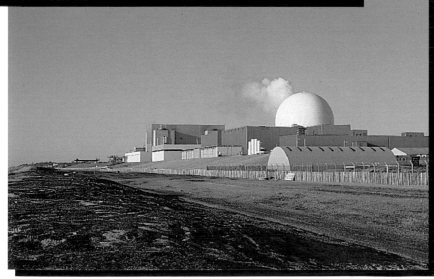

5

Photos on title page   Two nuclear power stations. The Sun has a power output of $4 \times 10^{26}\,\mathrm{W}$ and is fuelled by hydrogen in its core. In comparison, the $1.2 \times 10^9\,\mathrm{W}$ ($1\,200\,\mathrm{MW}$) of electrical power generated by the uranium-fuelled Sizewell B power station on the Suffolk coast is tiny. It would require 3×10^{17} such power stations to match the Sun's power output.

The Open University, Walton Hall, Milton Keynes MK7 6AA

First published 1998

Written, edited, designed and typeset by the Open University.

Printed and bound in the United Kingdom by Jarrold Book Printing, Norfolk, England.

ISBN 0 7492 8191 X

This text forms part of an Open University course, S103 *Discovering Science*. The complete list of texts that make up this course can be found on the back cover. Details of this and other Open University courses can be obtained from the Course Reservations and Sales Office, PO Box 724, The Open University, Milton Keynes MK7 6ZS, United Kingdom: tel. (0044) 1908 653231.

For availability of this or other course components, contact Open University Worldwide Ltd, The Berrill Building, Walton Hall, Milton Keynes MK7 6AA, United Kingdom: tel. (00 44) 1908 858585, fax (00 44) 1908 858787, e-mail ouwenq@open.ac.uk. Alternatively, much useful course information can be obtained from the Open University's website http://www.open.ac.uk

s103block5i1.1

Contents

1 **Introduction**   **5**

2 **Energy conversion and conservation**   **6**

   2.1 Summary of Section 2   8

3 **Work, energy and power**   **9**

   3.1 Force and work   9

   3.2 Kinetic energy   15

   3.3 Power   23

   3.4 Summary of Section 3   24

4 **Motion under gravity**   **25**

   4.1 Work done by gravity   26

   4.2 Work done against gravity — gravitational potential energy 27

   4.3 Gravitational energy and energy conservation   29

   4.4 Other forms of potential energy   32

   4.5 Summary of Section 4   33

5 **Energy in biological systems**   **34**

6 **Internal energy**   **36**

   6.1 What is internal energy?   36

   6.2 Specific heat — relating heat transfer to temperature change 39

   6.3 The absolute scale of temperature   40

   6.4 Latent heat of vaporization   41

   6.5 Summary of Section 6   44

7 **Electrical energy**   **45**

   7.1 Electric charge   45

   7.2 Conductors and insulators   46

   7.3 Electric current   48

   7.4 Electrical energy and voltage   49

   7.5 Electric power   50

   7.6 Summary of Section 7   51

8 **Energy from the Sun**   **52**

   8.1 Uses of solar energy   52

   8.2 The Earth's GMST — a final calculation   53

   8.3 Nuclear fusion — energy from the heart of the Sun   54

   8.4 Summary of Section 8   56

9   **Energy — an overview**   57

Questions: answers and comments   58

Acknowledgements   66

Index   67

Introduction

The term 'energy' has been used in each of the first four blocks in this course. In Block 1, it was mentioned in the context of the evaporation of water. In Block 2, you saw how the surface temperature of the Earth is determined by the rates at which it loses and gains energy. Among other things, Block 3 dealt with the energy available from the Sun and the release of energy during earthquakes. Finally, the controlled use of energy in various metabolic reactions, such as photosynthesis and respiration, was mentioned in Block 4 as one of the characteristics of life, and you saw the important part that was played by energy supplies and energy flows in the description of an oakwood ecosystem.

So far we have only introduced those ideas about energy that were necessary to understand particular topics. However, as we go on with the course this piecemeal approach will become less satisfactory. So, in this block we step aside from our quest to 'take the world apart' — our progression from the immense scale of the Universe (Block 3) to the subatomic scale of quarks (Block 7) — and we put the important concept of energy on a more secure footing. To do this, we need to think carefully about how energy is defined and how it can be calculated or measured. That is the purpose of this block.

The concept of energy in its precise, scientific sense is extraordinarily useful in every branch of science for two main reasons. First, almost all physical, chemical, biological and geological processes involve the *transfer* of energy between different locations, or between different objects, or its *conversion* into different forms. Second, these energy transfers and conversions take place according to a strict system of natural accountancy which states that after all changes have taken place, you always end up with exactly the same amount of energy as you started with. This law of conservation of energy is a very powerful tool, and we will exploit it to gain a deeper understanding of many areas of science.

In the next section (Section 2) we will discuss energy transfers and conversions in general terms. In Section 3, the relationship between force and energy will be explored, and we will show how this leads to the idea of the energy of motion. Sections 4–8 then deal with a variety of other forms of energy, including energy associated with gravity, with electricity, and with the Sun.

For a proper discussion of energy we will need to make extensive use of the mathematical tool of algebra that was introduced in Block 3. Please don't panic! Algebra is simply a language. It is a very precise and beautiful language, and it can describe mathematical ideas far more exactly and concisely than mere words. Like all languages, it has its own rules and grammar which have to be learned and practised; that learning can be slow, but is nevertheless very rewarding. Even if you have had difficulty with mathematics before, please bear with us. We hope that at the end of the block you will be astonished at your fluency in this strange tongue.

The main focus of skills development in this block is therefore algebra, but you will also be developing skills associated with problem solving, as well as other skills that have been introduced earlier in the course, particularly those associated with handling units and significant figures in calculations. In addition, there are activities that develop the important practical work skills of measuring, recording and analysing data, and critically evaluating results.

2 Energy conversion and conservation

When introducing the concept of energy in Block 2 (Box 4.1), we highlighted similarities between the everyday and scientific meanings of the word. Thus, if someone is described as being 'full of energy' or 'very energetic', it conjures up a picture of a person who is very active, works hard, moves around fast and probably accomplishes a lot (sickening, isn't it?). In science, the word 'energy' is also associated with speed of movement, activity and work, but it is much more precisely defined and appears in many different guises. Some of these you have already met, like the energy carried by electromagnetic radiation or the energy associated with chemical reactions. Others such as electrical energy or gravitational energy will be introduced later in this block. Indeed it might surprise you to know that matter itself is a form of energy and that this page, your own body and all other material objects in the Universe are nothing other than a form of energy! We will return to this in Section 8.

Energy can be transferred from one object to another. If you throw one of your S103 books up in the air (Figure 2.1), you transfer energy from the muscles in your arm and hand to the book, and ultimately to the floor (assuming you fail to catch the book). In this process energy is also converted from one form into another. It starts as *chemical energy* stored in the muscles of your arm. Chemical reactions associated with muscle contraction release some of this energy, and it is converted into energy of motion (called *kinetic energy*) of your hand and the book. As the book rises it slows down, and so its kinetic energy decreases. But the kinetic energy isn't destroyed; it is converted into a form of energy known as *gravitational energy* (about which we will have a lot more to say in Section 4). The gravitational energy of the book is converted back into kinetic energy as the book falls. When it strikes the floor it makes a noise (*sound energy*) and if you were to measure the temperature of the floor and the book after impact, with a very sensitive thermometer, you might record a slight increase in temperature in both. You may recall from Block 2 that an increase in the temperature of a substance is associated with an increase in the energy of its constituent molecules. We refer to the total energy of the constituent molecules as the *internal energy* of the substance.

Figure 2.1 Throwing an S103 book in the air involves a variety of energy transfers and conversions.

As another example, consider the energy transfers and conversions involved in making a cup of tea using an electric kettle (Figure 2.2). Chemical energy stored in the fuel at the power station is released when the fuel is burned, and is converted into internal energy in the steam which is used to turn the turbine (kinetic energy) driving the generator that produces *electrical energy*. The electrical energy is supplied to your house and converted into internal energy of the kettle element and then into internal energy of the water in the kettle, so the temperature of both increases. Some of this internal energy will be transferred to the kettle itself and to its surroundings, as well as to the tea cup and (eventually) yourself.

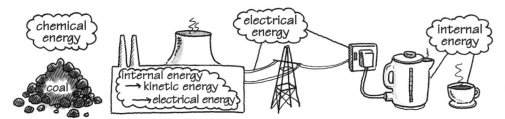

Figure 2.2 Energy transfers and conversions from chemical energy stored in coal to internal energy in a cup of tea.

In the examples just described, and in any other example you might care to think about, the **law of conservation of energy** rules. This means that the total amount of energy in all its different forms is *always* the same throughout any process, no matter what transfers or conversions take place. In the example of throwing a book up in the air, the book slows down as it rises and the *decrease* in its kinetic energy is balanced by the *increase* in its gravitational energy. The book speeds up as it falls and the *increase* in its kinetic energy matches the *decrease* in its gravitational energy, so that the total energy is always the same. Even after the book has come to rest on the floor, the increase in internal energy of the book and its surroundings will be exactly equal to the sum of the kinetic energy and the gravitational energy it had when it was thrown. In other words, energy is always conserved. This simple law appears to be true everywhere in the Universe and at all times, and we can summarize it as follows.

> The law of conservation of energy:
>
> In any process, the total amount of energy is always constant.
>
> Energy cannot be created or destroyed.

You may wonder how we know that this very general law applies everywhere and in all circumstances. For example, how can we possibly know whether the law of conservation of energy applies in the Andromeda Galaxy, some 10^{19} km from Earth (Figure 2.3)? Of course, no one has been to the Andromeda Galaxy — or is likely to go there — but we can put forward two very telling arguments in favour of our assertion. The first is that all experiments which have been carried out are consistent with the law of conservation of energy holding in all circumstances on Earth*, and there are no experimental results that disprove the law. The second is that, although we cannot go to Andromeda, we can observe it and other very distant objects. These observations are all consistent with the view that the laws of science are the same throughout the Universe — and the law of conservation of energy is one of the cornerstones on which the other laws of science rest.

Figure 2.3 The Andromeda Galaxy is about 10^{19} km from Earth, but astronomers are confident that the laws of science there are the same as they are on Earth.

* Actually, quantum theory (which you will discover in Block 7) suggests that, at the smallest scale, there is a slight degree of uncertainty in the energy accounting, but that is not relevant to discussions about the everyday world.

2.1 Summary of Section 2

Energy exists in a number of different forms. It can be converted from one form into another and transferred from one object to another or from one location to another.

The law of conservation of energy applies to *any* process in the Universe: the total amount of energy is *always* constant since energy is neither created nor destroyed.

Work, energy and power

So far we have been talking about energy transfers and conversions in a qualitative way, but in order to make measurements and calculations we need to think quantitatively. To do this we have to consider how energy can be measured and how it relates to other physical quantities.

The relationships between energy, in its various forms, and other quantities can best be expressed using algebra. We will develop your ability to understand and use this mathematical language in this section, but first it will be useful for you to review some basic ideas about algebra.

Activity 3.1   Reviewing the algebra introduced in Block 3

This activity gives you an opportunity to practise the skills associated with using symbols in equations that were developed earlier in the course. ◀

The symbols in an algebraic equation are rather like the words in a sentence. Each symbol has a specific meaning, and to make sense of an equation you have to know the meanings of the symbols, just as you have to know the meanings of the words to understand a sentence in a foreign language. As you study science, you will become familiar with the conventions that scientists use for representing particular physical quantities by particular symbols. For example, the volume of an object is usually represented by V and the speed at which light travels in a vacuum is always represented by the letter c. However, there are many quantities for which there is no agreed convention for the symbol used.

Generally scientists are careful to specify the meaning of the symbols that they use when they are writing books or research papers, and we are very careful to do this in S103. However, it is impractical to specify the meaning of a symbol every time it is used, and it would become extremely repetitive and boring if we did. So you will often come across a symbol whose meaning you are unsure of, and this can slow down your study of the course material. Also, when dealing with a variety of algebraic equations, as you will be while studying this block, you may find it difficult to remember the meaning of each equation.

Activity 3.2   Keeping track of symbols and equations

In this activity you will develop a strategy that will help you cope with the symbols and equations that you meet in this block. ◀

3.1   Force and work

Pushing a broken-down car along a road involves a lot of *work*, and it involves transferring a great deal of *energy* to the car. In this section we will discuss what scientists mean by work, how they measure it, and how it is related to energy and force.

We will start with an everyday example. Consider a child setting a toy train in motion along a track by giving it a push, as shown in Figure 3.1. To keep the example as simple as possible, we will make the following assumptions:

*   the train is initially stationary;

train initially stationary, no motor, no brakes, no friction

constant force applied by child

Figure 3.1 Pushing a train to set it in motion along a very long, straight, horizontal track.

- the train has no motor so that its motion is entirely dependent on the push given by the child;
- the track is straight and horizontal and very long;
- the train has no brakes and there is no friction anywhere within the moving parts of the train;
- the child provides a *constant* force for the length of time she is pushing the train.

Although these assumptions might seem unrealistic, they will prove to be very useful. It is often easier to grasp how things work by first thinking about the simplest possible situation. Once you have a clear picture of the simple case, you can gradually add in complications (to make it more realistic) and see what effect they have. This kind of 'thought experiment' has led to some very important scientific discoveries.

3.1.1 What is work?

In Block 3, you learned something about Newton's laws of motion. We can apply that knowledge to our toy train example.

○ Can you recall Newton's first law of motion?

○ Newton's first law states that an object will continue moving at constant speed in a straight line (or remain at rest) unless acted upon by an unbalanced force.

○ If the train is set in motion with a certain speed along the horizontal track, how long will it keep moving at the same speed?

○ If the train is truly frictionless and the track is horizontal, then there is no unbalanced force acting on the train and it will continue moving at the same speed until it reaches the end of the track.

Before it was pushed, the train was stationary; after the push it moves with a certain speed. Our intuitive ideas of energy would suggest that when the train is moving it must have *kinetic energy* — energy of motion — and this energy must increase as the speed of the train increases. It seems reasonable to assume that the kinetic energy was provided by the push, just as the kinetic energy of the book was provided by the throw in our earlier example (Figure 2.1). It also seems reasonable to assume that the greater the strength of the push, the greater the quantity of energy that is transferred to the train, since the train certainly travels faster.

The energy transferred to an object by a force is an important quantity and is given a special name. It is called the **work** done by the force on the object. The greater the force that is applied, the greater is the work done, and the greater the energy transferred to the object on which the force acts.

To express this idea mathematically, we need to write down an algebraic relationship linking the work done to the force applied. Just about the simplest assumption we could make is that the work done is proportional to the magnitude of the force, and measurements confirm that this assumption is indeed correct. In algebra, this is expressed using the proportionality symbol $\propto$ (Block 3, Box 12.1). Using the symbols W for work and F for the magnitude of the force, we can write:

$$W \propto F \tag{3.1}$$

If you assume that the proportionality relationship in Equation 3.1 is correct, what will happen to the amount of work done if the force is (a) doubled, or (b) divided by three?

(a) If the force is doubled, the work done will be doubled, and (b) if the force is divided by three, the work done will also be divided by three.

But the dependence of work on the force applied isn't the whole story. In a typically vigorous push, the child's hand might stay in contact with the train for, say, 20 cm. If she applied the same force but only stayed in contact with the train for 5 cm, the train would not travel as fast. So it seems that the energy transferred by the force increases when the distance over which the force is applied increases. We will use the symbol d to represent this distance, and again, our first assumption for the relationship between work W and distance d might be:

$$W \propto d \tag{3.2}$$

Again measurements confirm the validity of this assumption.

Here we have a situation where one quantity, work, is proportional to two other quantities. Can we write down a single expression that includes both relationships? The answer is yes. The work is simply proportional to the force F multiplied by the distance d over which the force is applied:

$$W \propto Fd \tag{3.3}$$

The reasoning behind this is shown in Box 3.1, *More about proportionality*, which develops further the ideas about proportionality introduced in Blocks 2 and 3.

Box 3.1   *More about proportionality*

Combining proportionalities

We can understand the proportionality between one quantity and two others by considering a rather trivial example. Suppose you buy several bars of chocolate in a supermarket and you want to work out how much they will cost. The total cost will be proportional to the number of bars you buy, and we will assume for simplicity that the cost of a bar is proportional to its mass. We can express this algebraically by using the symbols C for the total cost, N for the number of bars, and m for the mass of a bar.

Thus, the cost is proportional to the number of bars:

$$C \propto N$$

and the cost is proportional to the mass of each bar:

$$C \propto m$$

Can we now write down a relationship between C, N and m? Clearly the total cost is also proportional to the total mass of chocolate bought, which is the number of bars of chocolate (N) multiplied by the mass of each (m), and so:

$$C \propto Nm$$

We can summarize this result in a general way as follows. If a quantity a is proportional to each of a number of quantities b, c, d, that is, if:

$$a \propto b \text{ and } a \propto c \text{ and } a \propto d$$

then we can combine these relationships into the single proportionality relationship:

$$a \propto bcd$$

Constant of proportionality

A proportionality relationship can be converted into an equation by introducing what is known as a constant of proportionality. You probably use a 'constant of proportionality' every day without thinking about it.

We will return to the example of the chocolate bars. The relationship $C \propto Nm$ tells us that the cost C of the chocolate is proportional to the total mass of chocolate, Nm; that is if we double the mass of chocolate we buy then we double the cost. Supermarkets usually display the cost per unit mass of the products on their shelves (e.g. £2.59 per kg) and we can use this to write down an equation for the cost:

cost = cost per unit mass × mass of chocolate

If we use the symbol k to represent the cost per unit mass, then this equation becomes:

$C = kNm$

In general, any proportionality relationship can be turned into an equation by a similar process. The quantity k is known as the **constant of proportionality**. (You will meet a number of other constants of proportionality later in this block, some denoted by the symbol k and others by different symbols.)

The meaning of a constant of proportionality becomes clear if you make it the subject of the equation. Thus in the chocolate example, $C = kNm$, if we divide both sides of the equation by Nm we get:

$$\frac{C}{Nm} = \frac{kNm}{Nm}$$

so $\quad \dfrac{C}{Nm} = k \quad$ or $\quad k = \dfrac{C}{Nm}$

Since C is the cost of the chocolate, and Nm is the total mass, this equation confirms that k is the cost per unit mass.

The meaning of the relationship 3.3, $W \propto Fd$, is illustrated in Figure 3.2. However, although this relationship tells us something about how work is related to force and distance, it doesn't give enough information to enable us to do a calculation. We first have to convert the proportionality relationship into an equation.

Figure 3.2 If work W done is proportional to force F multiplied by distance d over which it is applied, then doubling either the force or the distance will double the work done.

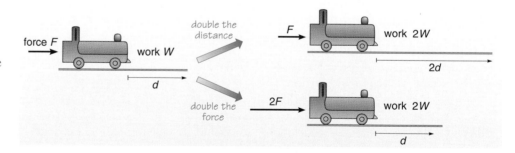

- How do you convert a proportionality relationship into an equation?

- This is done by introducing a constant of proportionality (Box 3.1).

So the proportionality relationship $W \propto Fd$ can be rewritten as:

$W = kFd$ (3.4)

where k is the constant of proportionality.

The constant k depends on the unit we use to measure the work done. However, recall that work is the name given to the energy transferred when a force acts on an object, so the unit of work is the same as the unit of energy. In the SI system, the unit of energy is *defined* so that the constant k has a value of one (and is simply a number with no units), and this means that:

1 SI unit of energy = 1 SI unit of force × 1 SI unit of distance   (3.5)

So if we use SI units we can rewrite Equation 3.4 as:

$$W = Fd \qquad\qquad (3.6)$$

○ Can you recall the SI units of energy (introduced in Block 2, Box 4.1) and force (introduced in Block 3, Section 4.2)?

○ The SI unit of energy is the joule, represented by the symbol J, and the SI unit of force is the newton, represented by the symbol N.

○ Use Equation 3.6 to write down a definition of the joule.

○ One joule is the energy transferred (or the work done) when a force of one newton acts for a distance of one metre.

$$1 \text{ joule} = 1 \text{ newton} \times 1 \text{ metre} \qquad \text{or} \qquad 1\,\text{J} = 1\,\text{N} \times 1\,\text{m} = 1\,\text{N m} \qquad (3.7)$$

You will discover how to calculate the amount of energy for various objects and situations later in the block, but to give you an idea of the size of a joule, it requires one joule to lift a 100 g object (a small apple, perhaps) through a distance of 1 m, and a 100 g object that is travelling at $5\,\text{m s}^{-1}$ (a good running speed) has a kinetic energy of about 1 J.

There is a refinement to the definition of work which we need to introduce here, and this is that the work done depends on the distance moved *in the direction in which the force is acting*. This is obvious if you consider once more the child pushing the train. If she pushes from the side, perpendicular to the direction of the track as in Figure 3.3, the train will not move in that direction (assuming that she does not push hard enough for the train to topple over). This is because the force she exerts is balanced by the force exerted by the track pushing back on the wheels. No energy is transferred to the train in this case — it is in exactly the same position as before the force was applied — and therefore no work is done on the train.

Figure 3.3 Pushing the train perpendicular to the direction of the track.

We can now provide a more precise definition of work as follows:

The work W done by a force on an object is the energy transferred to the object, and is equal to the magnitude F of the force multiplied by the distance d that the object moves in the direction of the force while the force is acting on it.

$$W = Fd \qquad\qquad (3.6)$$

3.1.2 Calculating the work done

The following example shows how we can calculate the work done on the train in Figure 3.1. Let's assume that the child pushes the train by applying a constant force of 2 N in the direction of the track over a distance of 0.3 m. The work done by the child on the train is calculated using Equation 3.6, $W = Fd$. We need to substitute the appropriate values of F and d into this equation: $F = 2\,\text{N}$, $d = 0.3\,\text{m}$. Thus:

$$W = 2\,\text{N} \times 0.3\,\text{m} = 0.6\,\text{N m}$$

Figure 3.4 Two Sumo wrestlers pushing against each other with equal and opposite forces.

But 1 N m = 1 J (Equation 3.7), and so the work done on the train is 0.6 J. Note that it would not be wrong to quote the answer as 0.6 N m, but it is conventional to use the simpler unit, the joule, for work done or energy transferred.

Question 3.1   Your car breaks down and you push it for a distance of 15 m by applying a force of 415 N in the direction in which the car is moving. How much work have you done on the car? ◀

Question 3.2   Two Sumo wrestlers push against each other with opposing forces of 1 200 N, and both remain stationary (Figure 3.4). How much work has been done on each wrestler? ◀

These two questions involved calculating the work done, and hence the energy transferred, when the force and the distance moved were known. In other circumstances we might wish to calculate the force needed to transfer a certain amount of energy, or the distance that must be travelled for a known force to do a certain amount of work. Such problems require the rearrangement of Equation 3.6. Box 3.2, *Rearranging and solving equations*, reminds you of some of the relevant skills you learned in Block 3, Box 3.1 and introduces a few more; you should study this before tackling Question 3.6.

Box 3.2   *Rearranging and solving equations*

It is often necessary to rearrange an equation to get it in a suitable form to calculate a particular quantity. For example, in Activity 3.1 you rearranged the equation $p = \dfrac{N}{A}$ to make A the subject, and you did this by first multiplying both sides of the equation by A to give $Ap = N$, and then dividing both sides by p to give $A = \dfrac{N}{p}$. You then substituted values of N and p into this equation to calculate the value of A. This whole process is referred to as *solving the equation* to find A.

The key to rearranging equations is that:

> if you carry out the same operation on both sides of an equation, then the two sides of the equation will still be equal.

The four main operations that can be carried out to rearrange equations are summarized in Table 3.1. For the sake of clarity, these examples use the same three symbols A, B and C, the meanings of which are unspecified, but later you will be able to try your hand

Table 3.1   Rearranging and solving equations.

To make B the subject of this equation	Carry out this operation on *both sides* of the equation	This gives the equation	Cancel Cs on the right of the equation	Swap left and right sides to end up with the equation for B
$A = \dfrac{B}{C}$	*multiply* by C	$A \times C = \dfrac{B}{C} \times C$	$A \times C = B$	$B = AC$
$A = BC$	*divide* by C	$\dfrac{A}{C} = \dfrac{BC}{C}$	$\dfrac{A}{C} = B$	$B = \dfrac{A}{C}$
$A = B - C$	*add* C	$A + C = B - C + C$	$A + C = B$	$B = A + C$
$A = B + C$	*subtract* C	$A - C = B + C - C$	$A - C = B$	$B = A - C$

at examples that relate to real scientific problems. You used the first two operations in Block 3 and in Activity 3.1, but the other two are introduced here for the first time.

The important points to notice about all of the ways of rearranging equations illustrated in Table 3.1 are that:

- the same operation is carried out on *both* sides of the equation in each example;
- the operation that we choose to use first is the one that cancels the unwanted quantity from one side of the equation, so:

  $/ C$ is cancelled by $\times C$

  $\times C$ is cancelled by $/ C$

  $- C$ is cancelled by $+ C$

  $+ C$ is cancelled by $- C$

In many situations you will have to choose a suitable combination of these operations to end up with the equation that you want.

Question 3.3   Newton's second law (Block 3) states that the magnitude F of the force on an object is equal to the mass m of the object multiplied by the magnitude of its acceleration a. This is expressed by the algebraic equation $F = ma$. Rearrange this equation to make the acceleration a the subject of the equation. ◀

Question 3.4   If a car accelerates steadily along a straight road from an initial speed u up to a final speed v in a time t, then the magnitude of its acceleration is

$$a = \frac{v - u}{t}$$

Rearrange this equation to make the final speed v the subject of the equation. ◀

Question 3.5   The larvae of blowflies (maggots) wriggle away from a source of light. Their speed of retreat v is given by the equation:

$$v = \frac{kI}{d^2}$$

where I is the intensity of the light source, d is the distance they are away from the light source, and k is a constant. Rearrange the equation to make I the subject of the equation. ◀

The following question requires you to rearrange Equation 3.6 as a first step in solving the problem posed.

Question 3.6   In 1957, the American strong man, Paul Anderson, set a world record that still stood 40 years later. He lifted a platform holding a total mass of 2 840 kg. In doing this, he exerted a force of 2.79×10^4 N and did 2.8×10^2 J of work on the platform. Through what distance did he raise the platform? ◀

3.2   Kinetic energy

In the last section, we said that kinetic energy was related to speed but we didn't say precisely how. We can now address that question. Our aim is to write down an algebraic equation for the kinetic energy of an object in terms of its speed and its mass. Our motivation for doing this is that once we have such an equation we will be able to calculate the kinetic energy of *any* object very easily.

To obtain the equation for the kinetic energy we will combine a number of different algebraic equations, each of which you have already met, either in Section 3.1 or in Block 3. This involves a procedure that is very similar to substituting values into an algebraic equation. The procedure is outlined in Box 3.3, *Combining algebraic equations*, and you should study this box carefully before continuing with Section 3.2.1.

Box 3.3 Combining algebraic equations

It is often necessary in science to combine two algebraic equations to produce a third equation that allows you to calculate a particular quantity. For example, you know from Block 3 that:

$$\rho = \frac{m}{V} \qquad \left(\text{i.e. density} = \frac{\text{mass}}{\text{volume}} \right)$$

and from Block 1, Box 4.2 that the volume (V) of a rectangular block is found from its length (l), its width (w) and its height (h), so:

$$V = lwh \qquad \text{(i.e. volume = length} \times \text{width} \times \text{height)}$$

If we wished to determine densities by measuring the masses and dimensions of blocks of materials, then it would be useful to have an equation that related ρ to m, l, w and h directly, and that didn't involve the volume V. We can find such an equation by making use of the fact that $V = lwh$. Since the two sides of any equation are equal (that's what we mean by an equation!), we can replace V by lwh in the equation for the density.

$$\rho = \frac{m}{V}$$

replace V by lwh

$$\rho = \frac{m}{lwh}$$

This process of replacing V by lwh is known as *substitution*; since we have substituted an equivalent quantity for V into the original equation, the new equation must still balance.

Here is another worked example. If a car accelerates in a straight line from rest for a time t, then the distance d that it travels is related to the magnitude of its acceleration, a, by the following equation (which you do not need to remember):

$$d = \tfrac{1}{2}at^2$$

The car's acceleration is related to its speed v after this time by:

$$a = \frac{v}{t}$$

Suppose that we want to know the distance travelled, and have measured the speed v and the time t. We can eliminate a from the first equation by substituting an equivalent quantity $\dfrac{v}{t}$ from the second equation. So:

$$d = \frac{1}{2}at^2$$

replace a by $\frac{v}{t}$

$$d = \frac{1}{2}\frac{v}{t}t^2$$

Since $t^2 = t \times t$, the t on the bottom of the fraction will cancel one of these ts, and the result is:

$$d = \tfrac{1}{2}vt$$

This equation allows us to calculate the distance d the car travels from rest, from the final speed v and the time t, without needing to know the value of the acceleration a.

Now try the following questions, which will give you some practice with substituting in algebraic equations.

Question 3.7 Suppose $x = \dfrac{2z^2}{a}$ and $a = 4zr$. Find an equation for x that does not involve a. ◀

Question 3.8 Suppose $y = 3t^2 + v$ and $t = 2z$. Find an equation for y that does not involve t. ◀

3.2.1 Finding an equation for kinetic energy — algebra in action

To discover the appropriate equation for kinetic energy we will work through a short 'thought experiment', during which we will assign algebraic symbols to all the important quantities. If this seems a little daunting — persevere. It demonstrates the power of algebra, and you are not expected to remember the steps that lead to the kinetic energy equation.

We start our thought experiment with a stationary train on a track, as illustrated in Figure 3.5. Now imagine that the child pushes the train with a constant force of magnitude F during which time the train moves a distance d. The push lasts for a time t, after which the train has a speed v and a kinetic energy E_k. In this block, we use the symbol E to represent energy and add different subscripts to differentiate between different kinds of energy. Thus the subscript 'k' means that the energy is 'kinetic'. You should read this as 'ee-sub-kay' or just 'ee-kay'.

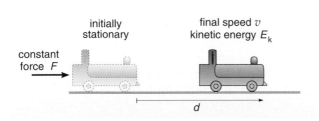

initially
stationary

final speed v
kinetic energy E_k

constant
force F

d

Figure 3.5   A train is pushed through a distance d by constant force F.

We assume once again that the track is horizontal and there is no friction in the moving parts of the train. So according to the law of conservation of energy, *all* of the work done by the child's push leads to an increase in the kinetic energy of the train. This means that:

kinetic energy of train = work done on train

or $E_k = W$ (3.8)

However, we already know that work is equal to force multiplied by distance, $W = Fd$, so we can substitute Fd in place of W in Equation 3.8, and write:

$E_k = Fd$ (3.9)

Now we want to find an equation that tells us how E_k depends on the mass m and speed v of an object, and that means we have to consider how the force F and distance d are related to these quantities. We'll start by considering the force F.

In Block 3, Section 4.2 you were introduced to Newton's second law of motion, and this tells us that, in our example, the magnitude F of the force is related to the mass m of the train and the magnitude a of its acceleration by the equation $F = ma$. This means we can substitute ma in place of F in Equation 3.9, and write:

$E_k = mad$ (3.10)

(Resist the temptation to read this equation as 'kinetic energy is mad'! You should read it as 'kinetic energy equals mass multiplied by acceleration multiplied by distance'.)

The next step is to relate the magnitude of the acceleration to the speed (as you did in Block 3, Section 4.1). Since the train is pushed with constant force, the acceleration is constant, and so the speed of the train increases steadily with time, as shown by the graph in Figure 3.6. For our train, travelling along the straight track, the magnitude of the acceleration a is the rate of change of speed, which means the change of speed divided by the time over which the change occurs. The graph shows that the speed changes from zero to v in a time t, so

$$a = \frac{v - 0}{t} = \frac{v}{t}$$

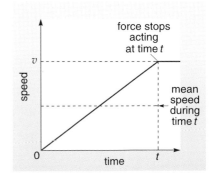

force stops
acting
at time t

v

speed

mean
speed
during
time t

0   time t

Figure 3.6   The speed v of the train shown in Figure 3.5 increases steadily for a time t while the constant force is acting on it.

Notice that, as the train is moving in a straight line, we don't have to worry about any acceleration associated with a change of direction. If we substitute $\frac{v}{t}$ in place of a in Equation 3.10, then it becomes:

$$E_k = m\frac{v}{t}d = mv \times \frac{d}{t} \tag{3.11}$$

As our aim is to find an equation for E_k that involves only v and m, we now want to replace the distance d and the time t in Equation 3.11, and this is why we have separated these two quantities from m and v on the right of the equation.

⬤ What is $\frac{d}{t}$ equal to?

◯ $\frac{d}{t}$ is distance travelled divided by time taken, and this is just the mean speed of the train during the time t.

During the time t, the speed of the train increases steadily from zero to its final speed v, as shown in Figure 3.6. So its mean speed is $\frac{(0 + v)}{2} = \frac{v}{2}$, which is half of the final speed.

But we said earlier that the mean speed was $\frac{d}{t}$, so we can write:

$$\text{mean speed} = \frac{d}{t} = \frac{v}{2}$$

This means that we can substitute $\frac{v}{2}$ in place of $\frac{d}{t}$ in Equation 3.11, and this leads to

$$E_k = mv \times \frac{v}{2} = \frac{mv^2}{2}$$

$$E_k = \tfrac{1}{2}mv^2 \tag{3.12}$$

Equation 3.12 achieves the goal we set at the beginning of the section. It expresses the **kinetic energy** E_k of an object — its energy of motion — in terms of its mass m and its speed v. And although we derived this equation for the particular case of a toy train, it is important to stress that the result is generally true. *Any* object with mass m that is moving at speed v has kinetic energy $\tfrac{1}{2}mv^2$.

Notice the benefit of working out the relationship using algebra. Equation 3.12 is packed with information. It not only allows us to calculate the kinetic energy of any object from its mass m and its speed v, but it also tells us exactly how the relationship works. For example, we can see at a glance that the kinetic energy is proportional to the mass, but depends on the *square* of the speed.

Let's take a specific example, and calculate the kinetic energy of a car, which has mass of 800 kg and is travelling at 20 m s^{-1} (72 km h^{-1}). We simply have to substitute $m = 800$ kg and $v = 20$ m s^{-1} into Equation 3.12. So:

$$E_k = \tfrac{1}{2} \times (800\,\text{kg}) \times (20\,\text{m s}^{-1})^2$$

$$= 400\,\text{kg} \times 400\,\text{m}^2\,\text{s}^{-2} = 1.6 \times 10^5\,\text{kg m}^2\,\text{s}^{-2} = 1.6 \times 10^5\,\text{J}$$

So the kinetic energy of the car is 1.6×10^5 J.

Now you may have noticed that we changed the unit of the answer from $\text{kg m}^2\,\text{s}^{-2}$ to J in the course of this calculation. These units are equivalent to one another, and this equivalence is explained in Box 3.4, *Getting the correct units*, which you should study now.

Box 3.4 Getting the correct units

We have stressed the importance of always quoting the units of values in calculations and answers. But how do you make sure that you've got the correct unit for the answer to a calculation?

With the variety of new units that we have introduced in this course you may think that this is quite tricky, particularly since you will often end up with strange combinations of units when substituting values in algebraic equations. Take the following calculation as an example:

$$F = ma = 10\,\text{kg} \times 2\,\text{m s}^{-2} = 20\,\text{kg m s}^{-2}$$

This answer does not have the SI unit that is conventionally used for force, the newton. However, you know from Block 3 that 1 N is *defined* as $1\,\text{kg m s}^{-2}$ so the answer above is equivalent to 20 N.

Here's a second example:

$$W = Fd = 5\,\text{N} \times 0.3\,\text{m} = 1.5\,\text{N m}$$

Here the answer for the work done is expressed in the unit N m, and although this is correct, work done is conventionally expressed in the SI unit of energy, the joule. However, 1 J is 1 N m (Equation 3.7) so the answer above is equivalent to 1.5 J.

So how do we ensure that we get the correct unit at the end of a calculation? There are two approaches.

1 Make sure that the values that you substitute into an equation are always expressed in the basic SI units. So always use m for distances, and not km or mm, and always use kg for masses, rather than g (remember, the basic SI unit for mass is kg, not g). *Then the unit of the answer will be the basic SI unit for the quantity calculated.*

Here are two examples:

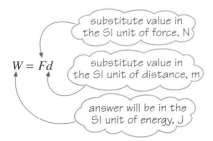

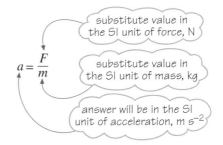

So if you remember the SI unit for each quantity, then it is straightforward to write down the unit of the answer.

2 The second approach involves keeping track of all of the units in equations, and substituting equivalent units where necessary to end up with the appropriate unit for the answer. This is the approach that we would recommend that you use when you are familiarizing yourself with new units. As with the first approach, you should make sure that the values that you substitute into an equation are expressed in the basic SI units. We used this approach in the two examples at the beginning of this box, and you may wish to read through these examples again now.

Of course, this second approach assumes that you remember the equivalencies between various units! However, these can always be deduced from a few basic equations. Thus:

$a = \dfrac{v}{t}$ tells us that the unit of acceleration is $\dfrac{\text{m s}^{-1}}{\text{s}}$, or m s^{-2}

$F = ma$ tells us that the unit of force, N, is equivalent to $1\,\text{kg} \times 1\,\text{m s}^{-2}$, or $1\,\text{kg m s}^{-2}$

$W = Fd$ tells us that the unit of energy, J, is equivalent to $1\,\text{N} \times 1\,\text{m}$, or $1\,\text{N m}$

You can then deduce other equivalent units by combining relationships like those above. For example, since:

$$1\,\text{J} = 1\,\text{N m, and } 1\,\text{N} = 1\,\text{kg m s}^{-2}$$

we can replace N in the first equation by $kg\,m\,s^{-2}$, to get:

$$1\,J = 1\,kg\,m\,s^{-2} \times m = 1\,kg\,m^2\,s^{-2}$$

and this is the relationship that we used in the worked example that followed Equation 3.12.

You may find it helpful to make a list of the equivalencies between different units as part of your glossary of symbols and equations (Activity 3.2).

Activity 3.3   How do you solve problems? Part I

In this activity you will answer a question and then review how you went about doing it. This will help you to develop general strategies that will be useful when you tackle more complex questions in this, and later, blocks. ◀

3.2.2   Using the kinetic energy equation

We can squeeze more information out of Equation 3.12 by rearranging it. For example, we can make v the subject of the equation so that we can calculate the speed if we know the kinetic energy and mass. To do this, we multiply both sides by 2 to cancel out the $\frac{1}{2}$, and divide both sides by m in order to cancel out the m on the right of the equation, and this gives:

$$E_k = \frac{1}{2}mv^2$$

$$E_k \times \frac{2}{m} = \frac{1}{2}mv^2 \times \frac{2}{m}$$

$$\frac{2E_k}{m} = v^2$$

$$v^2 = \frac{2E_k}{m} \tag{3.13}$$

We are almost there, but we have an expression for v^2, rather than for v itself. In order to write v as the subject of the equation, we need to 'take the square root' of both sides. This procedure is explained in Box 3.5, *Squares and square roots*.

Box 3.5   Squares and square roots

The **square** of a number is that number multiplied by itself. Thus the square of 5 means 5×5 and is written 5^2, and is spoken as 'five squared'; the square of x means $x \times x$ and is written as x^2, and is spoken as 'ex squared'. Also, from Block 1 you will be familiar with the unit of area, m^2; this is the square of m, that is $m \times m$, which is spoken as 'square metres' or 'metres squared'.

The square of any number is easily worked out using a calculator. You can multiply the number by itself in the same way that you would multiply any two numbers, but there is a quicker method that makes use of the $\boxed{x^2}$ key on scientific calculators. You may need to experiment with your calculator, or read the instruction booklet, to find out how to use it to calculate squares of numbers.

Often in science or mathematics, the situation arises where you know the value of the square of a number and you need to know the number itself. For example, you may wish to know the value of x, and be given the information that the square of x is 9. Using algebra, this would be written as:

$$x^2 = 9$$

Your problem is to find the number which when multiplied by itself is equal to 9. The phrase 'the number which when multiplied by itself' is rather long winded and so is given a special name, the **square root**, and is represented by the symbol $\sqrt{\ }$.

Thus 'the number which when multiplied by itself is equal to 9' is simply 'the square root of 9', and is written as $\sqrt{9}$. The process of finding this number is called 'taking the square root'.

If we follow the principle that we can do whatever we like to one side of an equation providing we do the same to the other side, then we can make x the subject of the equation $x^2 = 9$ by 'taking square roots' of both sides. The square root of x^2 must be simply x, so we get:

$$\sqrt{x^2} = \sqrt{9}, \text{ i.e. } x = \sqrt{9}$$

As you probably realize, $\sqrt{9} = 3$ (since $3 \times 3 = 9$), but for many other numbers the square root is not so easily worked out. Before the electronic age, square roots had to be calculated painstakingly by complicated arithmetical methods or looked up in tables. Now they can be conveniently found by the touch of a button on a calculator. Most scientific calculators have a square root key that automatically calculates the square root of the number in the display. This key is usually labelled with the square root symbol $\sqrt{\ }$. In some calculators, the number is keyed in first and then the $\boxed{\sqrt{\ }}$ key is pressed. So to find the square root of 156.5 you would key in the following:

$$\boxed{1}\,\boxed{5}\,\boxed{6}\,\boxed{.}\,\boxed{5} \text{ then } \boxed{\sqrt{\ }}$$

and the answer 12.509 996 would appear in the display, which is 12.51 to four significant figures. In other calculators the $\boxed{\sqrt{\ }}$ key is pressed *before* the number whose square root is required. You should check which way your calculator operates by using it to calculate $\sqrt{4}$ (= 2).

Square roots are also useful when rearranging or solving algebraic equations. For example, suppose that we have an equation:

$$v^2 = 2ad$$

and we want to know the value of v. We can take the square root of both sides of the equation:

$$\sqrt{v^2} = \sqrt{2ad}$$

But $\sqrt{v^2} = v$ (because $v^2 = v \times v$), so:

$$v = \sqrt{2ad}$$

(Note that in $\sqrt{2ad}$ the bar in the square root sign stretches across the $2ad$. This means 'the square root of $2ad$'. If the bar had stretched across only the 2, i.e. as in $\sqrt{2}ad$, this would have meant 'the square root of 2, multiplied by ad'. Therefore care needs to be taken when writing or reading $\sqrt{\ }$ signs.)

Question 3.9 (a) Use your calculator to work out the squares of 3.2, 17.4, 8.3 and 0.5, and express the answers to the same number of significant figures as in the original number.

(b) Use your calculator to work out the square roots of 80, 111, 1 015.3 and 0.5, and express the answers to the same number of significant figures as in the original number.

(c) Rearrange the equation $d = \frac{1}{2}at^2$ to make t the subject. ◀

We can now use square roots to convert the expression for v^2 in Equation 3.13,

$v^2 = \dfrac{2E_\text{k}}{m}$, into an expression for v instead. Taking the square root of both sides of the equation, we obtain:

$$v = \sqrt{\frac{2E_\text{k}}{m}} \tag{3.14}$$

This equation allows us to calculate the speed of an object if we know its kinetic energy and its mass.

Activity 3.4 How do you solve problems? Part II

In this activity you will use the strategy developed in Activity 3.3 to solve a different problem, and will review your strategy, and adapt and refine it. ◀

3.2.3 Re-examining our initial assumptions

Now that we have a clear picture of the relationship between force, work and kinetic energy in the simplest case, we can explore some of the assumptions we made at the beginning of Section 3.1.

What if the train is not stationary when the force is applied?

If the force is applied when the train is already moving (Figure 3.7), we can run through similar arguments to those in Section 3.2.1, but this time the *change* in kinetic energy is equal to the work done by the force. We represent the initial speed of the train by the symbol u, and the final speed by the symbol v. Then its initial kinetic energy is $\frac{1}{2}mu^2$, and its final kinetic energy is $\frac{1}{2}mv^2$, so the change in kinetic energy is $\frac{1}{2}mv^2 - \frac{1}{2}mu^2$. Equation 3.12 therefore becomes:

$$\text{change in } E_k = \frac{1}{2}mv^2 - \frac{1}{2}mu^2$$

Figure 3.7 Pushing a train that was initially moving with speed of u.

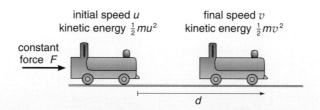

It is a little tedious to keep writing 'change in E_k' all the time. Fortunately there is a standard notation for representing changes in quantities, and this uses the Greek upper case letter Δ (**delta**) followed by the quantity. Thus:

Δx means 'the change in x', and is spoken as 'delta-ex'.

The 'change in E_k' can therefore be written as ΔE_k (spoken as 'delta-ee-sub-kay') and the equation finally becomes:

$$\Delta E_k = \frac{1}{2}mv^2 - \frac{1}{2}mu^2 \tag{3.15}$$

Note that ΔE_k does *not* mean Δ multiplied by E_k. In this case ΔE_k is treated as a single quantity.

Question 3.10 Calculate the work done on a toy train (Figure 3.7) of mass 200 g to increase its speed from an initial value of 1.0 m s^{-1} to a final value of 2.0 m s^{-1}. ◀

What if there is some friction involved?

For our toy train example, if frictional forces exist within the moving parts, some of the energy transferred to the train will be converted into internal energy. Applying the law of conservation of energy we can write:

$$\begin{pmatrix} \text{energy transferred} \\ \text{to train} \end{pmatrix} = \begin{pmatrix} \text{change in kinetic} \\ \text{energy of train} \end{pmatrix} + \begin{pmatrix} \text{change in internal} \\ \text{energy of train} \end{pmatrix}$$

or $W = \Delta E_k + \Delta E_i \tag{3.16}$

where we have used ΔE_i to represent the change in internal energy of the train.

The magnitude of this internal energy change depends on the frictional forces. If the friction between the moving parts increases, then more of the energy transferred to the train will be converted into internal energy. Consequently a smaller proportion of the energy transferred to the train will be converted into kinetic energy, so the train's speed will be slower.

Question 3.11   Assuming that there are frictional forces between the parts of the train, describe what happens to the speed of the train, and to the energy of the train, after the child has completed her 'push'. ◀

What if the track isn't horizontal?

If the track is horizontal, then the force of gravity is perpendicular to the direction of motion. From the definition of work in Section 3.1, you can see that the force of gravity does no work on the train and therefore has no effect on its kinetic energy. If the track is not horizontal, then the effect of the force of gravity will need to be taken into account. That is the subject of Section 4.

3.3   Power

So far in this block we have been mainly concerned with calculating amounts of energy converted from one form to another, but it is often useful to know the *rate* at which energy is converted (or transferred). You will recall from Block 2 (Box 4.1) that this is known as *power*. The power P can be calculated by dividing the energy converted, E, by the time t taken to do the conversion.

$$P = \frac{E}{t} \qquad\qquad (3.17)$$

In the SI system of units, power is measured in joules per second, or *watts*; the symbol for the watt is W, so

$1\,\mathrm{W} = 1\,\mathrm{J\,s^{-1}}$

○ Suppose that the child in Figure 3.1 transferred 0.6 J of energy to the toy train when she pushed it. What additional information do you need in order to calculate the power involved in this energy transfer?

○ You need to know the *time* over which the energy was expended.

In this example, if the work was done by the child in 0.2 seconds, then the mean power over that time was:

$$P = \frac{E}{t} = \frac{0.6\,\mathrm{J}}{0.2\,\mathrm{s}} = 3\,\mathrm{J\,s^{-1}} = 3\,\mathrm{W}$$

Note, that if we know the total energy converted in a given time, all we can calculate is the *mean* power used during that time. There might be all kinds of fluctuations about the mean value — but we have no way of knowing that. However for many purposes, the mean power used in a given time is a very useful quantity.

Question 3.12   In Question 3.1 you calculated that the work done in pushing a car with a force of 415 N for a distance of 15 m is 6.2×10^3 J. If it took 30 seconds to push the car this far, calculate the mean power involved. ◄

Question 3.13   A stationary golf ball of mass 5.0×10^{-2} kg is struck by a club, which gives it a speed of 80 m s^{-1}. If the mean power used during the contact between club and ball is 3.1 kW, calculate the length of time for which ball and club are in contact. ◄

3.4   Summary of Section 3

The work W done by a force on an object is equal to the magnitude F of the force multiplied by the distance d that the object moves in the direction of the force while the force is acting on it, i.e. $W = Fd$.

The work done on an object is equal to the energy transferred to that object.

The SI unit of energy is the joule; $1 \text{ J} = 1 \text{ N} \times 1 \text{ m} = 1 \text{ N m} = 1 \text{ kg m}^2 \text{ s}^{-2}$.

If an object with mass m is moving with speed v, then its energy of motion, known as the kinetic energy E_k, is given by $E_k = \frac{1}{2}mv^2$.

Power P is the rate at which energy E is converted or transferred, and is given by $P = \dfrac{E}{t}$. The SI unit of power is the watt; $1 \text{ W} = 1 \text{ J s}^{-1}$.

Solving an equation often requires it to be rearranged. This can be done by performing identical operations on both sides of the equation, and/or by substituting an algebraic relationship obtained from another equation.

If $a \propto b$, and $a \propto c$ also, then $a \propto bc$. We can also say that $a = kbc$, where k is a constant of proportionality.

It is important to quote the correct unit with any quantity. If you substitute values into an equation in the correct SI units, then the unit of the answer will be the basic SI unit of the quantity calculated.

The square root of a quantity is the number (or expression) which when multiplied by itself is equal to the quantity.

Activity 3.2   Keeping track of symbols and equations (continued)

Before starting Section 4, you should make sure that you have included the important symbols, equations and units introduced in Section 3 in your personal glossary. This activity will help you to identify which of them are important. ◄

Motion under gravity

4

In Block 3 you were introduced to the gravitational force of attraction between objects. You also learned that this force is the reason you feel yourself pulled towards the Earth.

⬤ How does the magnitude of the gravitational force between two objects change when the masses of the objects increase, and when their separation increases?

◯ The magnitude of the gravitational force *increases* when the masses of the objects increase, and it *decreases* as their separation increases (Block 3, Section 4.3).

The gravitational force that you experience depends on the mass of the Earth, and on the separation between you and the mass of the Earth. For a large (approximately) spherical object like the Earth, it is the separation between you and the centre of the Earth that is relevant, and this separation is essentially the same for all objects close to the Earth's surface.

⬤ Does this mean that every object on the Earth's surface experiences the same gravitational force?

◯ No! The force experienced also depends on the mass of the object.

In fact, the gravitational force F_g experienced by an object is *proportional* to its mass m (Figure 4.1), so we can write:

$$F_g \propto m$$

Thus the force of gravity you experience due to the Earth is proportional to your own mass. Someone with a mass of 50 kg experiences only half the gravitational force felt by someone with a mass of 100 kg.

⬤ How can we express this relationship between gravitational force and mass as an algebraic equation?

◯ We can change a proportionality relationship between two quantities into an equation by introducing a constant of proportionality (Box 3.1).

In this case, the equation linking the gravitational force F_g with the mass m that experiences the force can be written as:

$$F_g = \text{constant} \times m \tag{4.1}$$

To discover the meaning of the constant in this equation, let's consider the motion of an object of mass m that is falling towards the Earth, for example, an apple falling from a tree. Newton's second law of motion states that the acceleration a of the object is related to the unbalanced force F acting on it by the equation:

$$F = m \times a \tag{4.2}$$

We will assume that the force due to air resistance is very small, and can be neglected, so that the object falls freely, acted on by only the gravitational force F_g. So the unbalanced force F in Equation 4.2 must be F_g. Therefore we can rewrite Newton's second law for a freely-falling object as:

$$F_g = m \times a \tag{4.3}$$

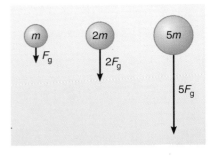

Figure 4.1   Gravitational force is proportional to mass.

Figure 4.2 Galileo's experiment, showing that cannonballs with different mass are accelerated equally by gravity. Historians doubt that Galileo performed this experiment, though he certainly did propose that gravity pulls large and small objects towards the Earth with the same acceleration. His proposal was so contentious at the time that he was forced to leave the University of Pisa.

We now have two equations for F_g, 4.1 and 4.3, and so we can equate the right-hand sides as follows:

$$m \times a = \text{constant} \times m \tag{4.4}$$

If we divide both sides of this equation by m, this leads to an important conclusion about the acceleration a of an object acted on by the force of gravity alone:

$$a = \text{constant} \tag{4.5}$$

> The **acceleration due to gravity** experienced by *any* object that is falling freely close to the Earth's surface is a constant. It has the same value, *irrespective of the mass of the object*.

This was the surprising result discovered about 400 years ago by Galileo, who is alleged to have dropped two cannonballs of different mass from the top of the Leaning Tower of Pisa and observed that they took approximately the same time to reach the ground (Figure 4.2).

The value of the acceleration due to gravity is always represented by the symbol g. It actually increases by about 0.5% between the Equator and the poles, and there are two reasons for this; one is the slightly non-spherical shape of the Earth and the other is the Earth's rotation. However, for the purpose of this course, we will usually ignore this small variation and will take the value of the acceleration due to gravity near to the Earth's surface to be $9.8 \, \text{m s}^{-2}$.

Question 4.1 What is the force due to gravity acting on (a) a person of mass 80 kg, and (b) a 100 g bar of chocolate? ◀

The gravitational force F_g experienced by an object is called the **weight** of the object. Now we showed that when an object is acted on by the force of gravity F_g alone, then its acceleration is g, the acceleration due to gravity. So according to Newton's second law:

$$F_g = mg \qquad \text{or} \qquad \text{weight} = mg \tag{4.6}$$

Note that, whereas the *mass m* of an object is constant (provided it does not lose or gain matter), its *weight F_g* is the gravitational force it experiences — and this depends on where on Earth (Figure 4.3) or in the Universe the object is located.

Question 4.2 What is the weight of a person with a mass of 80 kg (a) on the Earth (assuming $g = 9.8 \, \text{m s}^{-2}$), and (b) on the Moon where the acceleration due to gravity is roughly $1.6 \, \text{m s}^{-2}$? ◀

4.1 Work done by gravity

We can apply the ideas of Section 3 to calculate the work done on a falling object by the gravitational force. We will adopt the same simplifying approach as we did in Section 3, and start by making the assumption that air resistance is negligible. This is similar to our assumption of zero friction in the toy train example. In fact, air resistance *is* negligible for many practical purposes, so our calculations here won't be too unrealistic.

From the definition of work in Section 3.1, you should be able to see that if an object falls a certain distance, work will be done on it by the gravitational force that is acting on it. This work will cause the kinetic energy of the object to increase as it falls, just as the work done on the train caused its kinetic energy to increase. It is easy enough to calculate the energy involved. If we take as an example this book falling from a table onto the floor, as illustrated in Figure 4.4, we simply need to know the force (which is the weight of this book) and the distance travelled in the direction of the force (which is the height of the table).

○ Suppose that this book has a mass m, and the table top is a distance h above the floor. Write down an equation for the work W done by gravity on the book as it falls from the table top to the floor.

○ Work done $W = Fd$. In this case the force on the book is the weight, so $F = F_g = mg$, and the distance moved is the table height, so $d = h$. Thus:

$$W = mgh \qquad (4.7)$$

Question 4.3 (a) *Estimate* the work done on this book by gravity if you let it fall from your table to the floor. (Box 4.1, *Estimating*, contains advice on how to tackle this sort of question.)

(b) Assuming that air resistance is negligible, what is the kinetic energy of the book just before it hits the floor, and what is its speed at this point?

(c) What happens to this kinetic energy when the book hits the floor? ◀

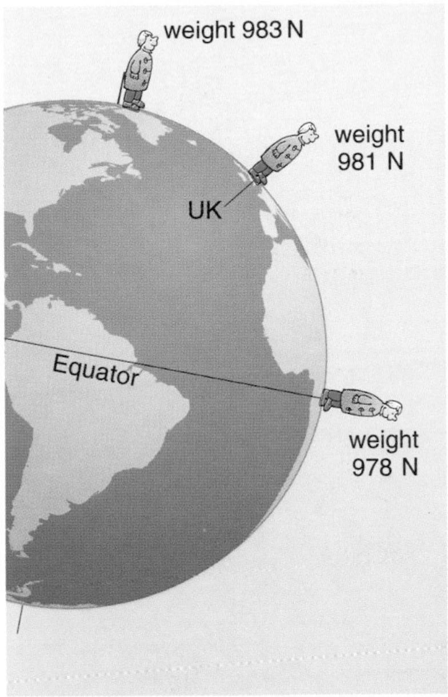

Box 4.1 Estimating

In Question 4.3a, you are asked to 'estimate' the work done when this book falls to the floor and to do this you need to use estimates of the mass of this book and the height of your table. That means you are not expected to use exact measured values, but rather to make educated guesses. For example, you might pick up this book and think how its mass compares with that of a 1 kg bag of sugar, or a 100 g pot of yoghurt, or the mass of some other object. Similarly you could compare the height of the table with your own height. You would also round the value of g to $10 \, \text{m s}^{-2}$, since your estimates of mass and height will only justify quoting the estimated work done to one significant figure.

Estimating is a useful skill to acquire as it gives you practice at doing rough calculations. By making sensible estimates with approximate values you can get a feel for the size of units like the joule and the newton. It is often useful to check the computations of your calculator (and the accuracy of your key pressing) by making rough calculations with approximate values, as we advised in Block 1.

4.2 Work done against gravity — gravitational potential energy

So far we have only considered objects falling under gravity. Let's now consider the work done when we lift an object. In order to lift an object that has mass m, we have to apply an upward force mg to overcome the downward force of gravity. If this force raises the object through a height h, then the work done is:

$$W = Fd = mg \times h = mgh$$

Figure 4.3 The small variation of the acceleration due to gravity with latitude means that the weight of a 100 kg person depends on their location on Earth. At all three locations the person's weight is 980 N (and $g = 9.8 \, \text{m s}^{-2}$) to two significant figures.

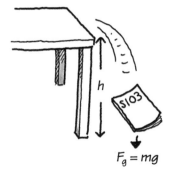

Figure 4.4 A falling book.

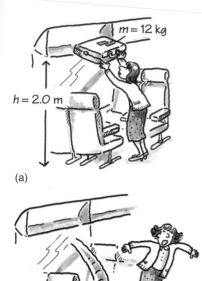

(a)

(b)

Figure 4.5 (a) Placing a suitcase on a luggage rack involves doing work against gravity. (b) The stored energy is released if the suitcase falls off the rack.

So if an object of mass m is raised through a height h, the work done on the object is equal to mgh, and so this amount of energy is transferred to the object. (Notice that this equation is identical to the one describing an object falling under gravity, Equation 4.7.)

Of course, this ties in very well with everyday observations. If you lift a heavy suitcase onto a luggage rack in a train, or a heavy bag of shopping onto a table, you are very aware that you are doing work against gravity. You will also be aware that more work is required to lift a more massive object, or the same object to a greater height, and these 'observations' are consistent with the work done being equal to mgh.

○ Calculate the work done in lifting a 12 kg suitcase from floor level up to a luggage rack 2.0 m above the floor (Figure 4.5a).

○ The work done is $W = mgh$, so

$$W = 12\,\text{kg} \times 9.8\,\text{m s}^{-2} \times 2.0\,\text{m}$$
$$= 235.2\,\text{kg m}^2\,\text{s}^{-2} = 240\,\text{J (to two sig figs)}$$

You might wonder what has happened to the 240 J of energy that was supplied to the suitcase to lift it onto the luggage rack. According to the law of conservation of energy, energy can't just disappear. When work was done on the toy train in Section 3, the energy supplied was converted into kinetic energy (and some internal energy when friction was taken into account), yet a suitcase placed on a luggage rack is obviously stationary. So where has the energy gone?

This question may be answered by considering what happens if the suitcase falls from the rack. As it falls, the energy reappears as kinetic energy, and the instant before it hits the floor all of the 240 J will be present as kinetic energy (Figure 4.5b). In other words, when the suitcase was lifted, energy was stored, ready to be released as kinetic energy when the case falls back down.

In general, when an object is raised to a greater height, work is done on the object and the energy transferred is stored; the amount of energy stored is $mg\Delta h$, where Δh is the change in height. This stored energy is given the name of *gravitational potential energy*. The term 'potential' signifies that this energy has the 'potential' for doing work when the object is lowered. However, as gravitational potential energy is a bit long-winded we will usually omit the 'potential' and refer to this energy just as **gravitational energy** E_g. You will meet other forms of potential energy later in this block.

Now in all problems that involve gravitational energy it is the *changes* of gravitational energy that are important. A *change* of height leads to a *change* of gravitational energy; the absolute value of the gravitational energy is unimportant. So if we drop our 12 kg suitcase through 2 m in a room at the top of a tower block, it will have the same kinetic energy, and the same speed, just before it hits the floor as if it falls 2 m from the luggage rack to the floor of a train. And in neither case can we say that the suitcase has no gravitational energy after falling, since we could push it off a balcony, or out of the train, and its gravitational energy would decrease as it fell further.

We can emphasize the importance of these changes by writing an equation for gravitational energy in terms of changes. Thus:

change in gravitational energy = $mg \times$ change in height

or if we use the Δ (delta) notation which we introduced in Section 3.2.3:

$$\Delta E_{\mathrm{g}} = mg\Delta h \tag{4.8}$$

Remember that ΔE_{g} means 'the change in E_{g}', and Δh means 'the change in h'. Clearly when an object is raised to a greater height, its gravitational energy increases, and when it falls to a lower height, then its gravitational energy decreases.

4.3 Gravitational energy and energy conservation

The concept of gravitational energy greatly simplifies calculations concerned with the effect of gravity on the motion of objects, particularly where no other forces are concerned. For example, if you take your book (which by now is getting rather dog-eared) and throw it vertically upwards in the air, it will slow down as it travels higher, and eventually reach a point where it is momentarily stationary. It will then accelerate downwards to where you (hopefully) catch it before it hits the ground. By using the idea of the change in gravitational energy, coupled with the law of conservation of energy, we can calculate such quantities as the speed of the book at a given height and the maximum height it will reach. These calculations assume that no air resistance acts on the book after it is thrown, so, in accordance with the law of conservation of energy, the sum of its kinetic energy and its gravitational energy must be constant. To say the same thing in another way — any increase in gravitational energy will be accompanied by a decrease in kinetic energy of equal size, and vice versa.

This will become clearer if we take a specific example. A book of mass m is thrown vertically upwards with an initial speed u. After it has risen through a height Δh it has a speed v.

○ What is the increase in gravitational energy of the book?

○ From Equation 4.8, the increase in gravitational energy is equal to $mg\Delta h$.

○ What is the *decrease* in kinetic energy of the book?

○ The book's initial kinetic energy is $\frac{1}{2}mu^2$ and its final kinetic energy is $\frac{1}{2}mv^2$ (from Equation 3.12); so the decrease in kinetic energy is $\frac{1}{2}mu^2 - \frac{1}{2}mv^2$. (Note that this is a *decrease* in kinetic energy, since the initial speed u is greater than the final speed v.)

Since energy is conserved, the increase in gravitational energy must be equal to the decrease in kinetic energy, so we can write down the following equation:

$$mg\Delta h = \frac{1}{2}mu^2 - \frac{1}{2}mv^2$$

Of course this equation doesn't apply only to books; it also applies to the movement of any object when gravity is the only force acting on it.

Activity 4.1   How do you solve problems? Part III

This is the third activity in which you will solve a problem, and then think about how you went about it so that you can further develop your strategy for solving problems. ◀

Figure 4.6   An unsuccessful attempt to rescue a damsel in distress.

25 m

Question 4.4   (a) An archer is trying to rescue a damsel in distress by firing an arrow, with a rope attached, vertically upwards to her lonely turret at a height of 25 m above him (Figure 4.6). Calculate the speed with which the arrow must be released to *just* reach the damsel. (To simplify things, you should assume that the rope is a magic one, which is very strong but has no mass so that its energy changes can be ignored!)

(b) If the damsel fails to catch the arrow, calculate the speed it will have when it returns to its starting point. ◀

Question 4.4 involved manipulating algebraic equations, and Box 4.2, *Manipulating algebra in problems*, gives some general advice about this.

Box 4.2   Manipulating algebra in problems

In the answer to Question 4.4, you may have noticed that we started with the equation:

$$mg\Delta h = \tfrac{1}{2}mu^2$$

and rearranged it to give:

$$u = \sqrt{2g\Delta h}$$

before substituting the numerical values. This strategy of combining and rearranging equations to make the required quantity the subject before substituting numerical values was recommended in Activity 4.1, and it is good practice in algebraic problems for the following reasons.

1   It is easier to see mistakes. If you substitute a lot of numbers and units into the original equation, and then try to rearrange it, it is very easy to lose track of where you are in the calculation. If you make an error, it is often very difficult to spot. When you do the rearrangement using the algebraic symbols, it is much easier to trace back through your answer and identify any errors.

2   It is easier to see how one quantity depends on another. For example, in Question 4.4, you can see that the initial speed is proportional to the square root of the maximum height.

3   Some symbols or numbers may cancel out when equations are rearranged, thus simplifying the final calculation. For example, the *m*s cancelled out in Question 4.4.

4 Having arrived at the final algebraic equation, it is very easy to repeat the calculation with different numerical values. If you substitute your numerical values first, you have to start the calculation afresh every time.

So you should generally rearrange algebraic equations *first*, and only substitute numerical values as the *last* stage of a calculation. Substituting numerical values earlier is not *wrong*, and if you do this you can still get the correct answer. However, it is best to substitute later if you can, for all of the reasons given above.

Question 4.5   A skier starts on a downhill run from an altitude of 2 500 m with an initial speed of 10 m s^{-1} and follows the path shown in Figure 4.7 until she reaches an altitude of 2 400 m. What is her final speed at the end of the run, assuming air resistance and friction between the skis and the snow can be neglected? ◀

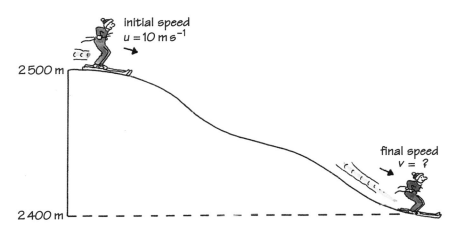

Figure 4.7   The path followed by the skier in Question 4.5.

Another common example of conversion between kinetic energy and gravitational energy is a child's swing, as illustrated in Figure 4.8a.

● At which point(s) during the motion of the swing will the gravitational energy have a maximum value, and at which point(s) will it have a minimum value?

○ The gravitational energy must be at a maximum at the two highest points of the swing cycle and at a minimum at the lowest point of the cycle (these points are shown in Figure 4.8a).

● At which points(s) during the motion of the swing will the kinetic energy have a minimum value, and at which point(s) will it have a maximum value?

○ Kinetic energy will be at a minimum value when the speed is at a minimum. This will occur at the highest points in the swing cycle, where the swing stops momentarily before reversing direction. Conversely, kinetic energy will be at a maximum when the speed is greatest — which is at the lowest point in the swing cycle shown in Figure 4.8a.

Alternatively we can use the law of conservation of energy to answer the previous question. If friction and air resistance are negligible, then the total energy is the sum of the kinetic energy and the gravitational energy, and this must be constant because energy is conserved. So the kinetic energy will be at a maximum when the gravitational energy is at a minimum and vice versa. This leads to exactly the same conclusion that we reached based on our experience of how the speed of a swing varies.

(a)

(b)

Figure 4.8   (a) Motion of a swing during its swing cycle. The swing is shown at the two highest points of its motion and at the lowest point. (b) An extra energy input is needed to combat the effects of friction.

31

Figure 4.9 This huge pendulum bob was suspended from the dome of St. Paul's Cathedral in London for an Open University television programme. Presented by Professor Mike Pentz, who is seen on the left and was first Dean of Science at the University, the programme demonstrated that the plane in which the pendulum swung actually rotated relative to the Cathedral, because of the daily rotation of the Earth. Using a massive pendulum bob reduced the proportion of the energy of the pendulum that was converted into internal energy by air resistance forces during each swing, so the pendulum continued to swing freely for a long time.

If there is no friction or air resistance gradually converting the available energy into internal energy, the swing would go backwards and forwards for ever, converting gravitational energy into kinetic energy and back again. However, for any real swing, there is always friction at the point of suspension, as well as air resistance during the swing's motion. Thus some of the kinetic energy will be converted into internal energy in the swing and its surroundings. For this reason a swing always comes to a halt in the absence of external forces — which is why parents are often employed to provide extra energy to maintain the swing's motion (Figure 4.8b).

The above discussion applies equally well to the motion of a pendulum. The conversion of kinetic energy into internal energy due to frictional forces can be made relatively very small by using a pendulum bob with a very large mass and suspending it from a very long cable.

Question 4.6 Figure 4.9 shows an enormous pendulum in St. Paul's Cathedral, London. The pendulum bob had a mass of 80 kg, the suspension cable was 82 m long, and the bob swung back and forth through a distance of 6 m. If the height difference between the highest and lowest points in the bob's motion is 5.5 cm, calculate (a) the change in gravitational energy of the bob between these points, and (b) the maximum speed reached by the bob. ◄

4.4 Other forms of potential energy

It is worth emphasizing that the gravitational energy (or gravitational potential energy, to give it the full name) of an object *increases* when it moves in the *opposite* direction to the gravitational force (i.e. when it moves upwards). This relationship between energy and force does not apply only to gravity. For many forces, motion *against* the force (that is, in the opposite direction to the force) allows energy to be stored, and this energy can be reclaimed when the object is allowed to move in the direction of the force. We refer to these types of energy as **potential energy** because the object has the potential to do work if it is allowed to move in the direction of the force.

An important example of potential energy is the energy stored within an object when it is stretched, or squashed or otherwise deformed. This kind of potential energy is called strain potential energy (or **strain energy** for short), and it finds uses in all kinds of devices from the spring in a clock to the rubber band in a catapult.

If you compress a spring, you do work against the force that the spring exerts to try and maintain its natural length. The energy stored in the spring depends on the change in length of the spring — or, alternatively, on the distance that the end of the spring is moved relative to its natural, undeformed position (see Figure 4.10). When you release the spring, the stored strain energy is converted into kinetic energy.

Figure 4.10 (a) A spring in its natural, undeformed state. (b) When work is done to compress the spring, energy is stored in the spring as strain energy. (c) When the spring is released, strain energy is converted into kinetic energy.

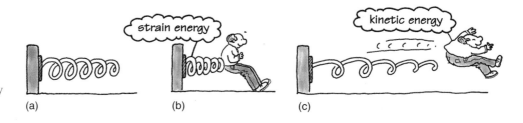

(a) (b) (c)

The distinguishing feature of potential energy in all its forms is that it depends on the *position* of an object and not on its motion. Thus gravitational (potential) energy depends on the height of an object, and strain (potential) energy depends on the compression (or extension) of an object. Other forms of potential energy will be discussed in Sections 6 and 7.

4.5 Summary of Section 4

All objects, irrespective of their mass, experience the same acceleration g when falling freely under the influence of gravity at the same point on the Earth. Close to the Earth's surface, $g = 9.8 \, \mathrm{m \, s^{-2}}$. The weight of an object is the force F_g due to gravity acting on the object, and for an object with mass m the weight is given by $F_g = mg$.

If the height of an object of mass m changes by Δh, the change in gravitational energy is $\Delta E_g = mg\Delta h$.

If gravity is the only force acting on an object, the sum of kinetic energy and gravitational energy is constant. Increases in kinetic energy are balanced by decreases in gravitational energy, and vice versa.

There are various forms of potential energy, all of which depend on the position of an object rather than on its motion. The potential energy of an object increases as it moves in the opposite direction to that of the force acting on it. Strain energy depends on the extension or compression of an object.

Energy in biological systems

The toy train which formed the basis of the discussion in Section 3 remains stationary unless work is done on it by a force. Under the action of a force, the train is set in motion, and the kinetic energy of the train is equal to the work done, provided friction doesn't cause some energy to be converted into internal energy.

Now when you begin to get up from studying this book to make a cup of tea or coffee, or to go to the pub, you will suddenly possess kinetic energy, and if you stand up from a seated position you will increase your gravitational energy. You will almost certainly be moving under your own volition without the action of an external force (except the psychological attraction of caffeine or alcohol). But the law of conservation of energy states that this energy cannot have arisen out of nowhere, so where did it come from?

A full answer to this question is complex and it will be tackled in more detail in Block 9. However, the simple answer is that you, along with all other living organisms, have stores of chemical energy which allow life processes to be carried out. For example, you have muscles which contract and relax as certain chemical reactions take place within them. Some of the energy released by these chemical reactions is converted into kinetic energy, which can propel you at great speed towards the kitchen or the pub or wherever your destination happens to be.

If you want to go one step further back and ask where the stored chemical energy that fuels muscular activity comes from, the answer is that it is present as stored chemical energy in the food you eat. This energy is transferred to your own internal chemical energy stores when the food is digested and its products are assimilated into the cells in your body.

The taking in of energy in the form of food, which can later be converted into other, more useful forms of energy, is a process common to all animals. We are made aware of this every time we go shopping, because many packaged foods carry a label giving their energy content. Thus an ice cream label that states that the energy content is 1 050 kJ per 100 g means that 1.05×10^6 J of energy are provided to your body when you consume 100 g of ice cream.

Question 5.1   Mrs Jones, whose mass is 60 kg, leaves her fourth-floor flat and descends 52 steps, each 0.18 m high, to go to a local shop for an ice-cream cornet. On her return, she takes a lick and consumes 5 g of the ice cream. If you assume that all of the energy stored in that quantity of ice cream could be converted into the gravitational energy of Mrs Jones, would this be enough to get her up the stairs to her flat? ◄

When you use your muscles, not all of the energy released in the chemical reactions is converted into kinetic energy or gravitational energy, or allows you to do useful work. Some is converted into internal energy that is associated with a rise in temperature of your body and this is why you get warm when you exercise. Your body's built-in control mechanisms then increase the flow of blood to the skin and initiate sweating to get rid of that extra internal energy before your body temperature rises too high. But even when you are resting, your body still has to release stored chemical energy to keep your body temperature close to the normal value of about 37 °C, and to maintain the various metabolic processes that are continually taking place throughout your body. For an average adult, the energy conversion rate while resting is about 75 W, equivalent to the power of an ordinary light bulb.

Chemical energy will be discussed further in Block 8 and the use of energy by biological systems is dealt with in Block 9. But to round off this section on energy in biological systems, and to link it to the earlier sections about kinetic energy and gravitational energy, you should do the following activity.

Activity 5.1   Conservation of energy during a locust's jump

In this activity you will investigate energy conversions and transfers in the jump of a locust. This will provide further practice with making, recording and analysing measurements, and with calculating changes in kinetic energy and gravitational energy. ◀

6 Internal energy

In almost every practical example of energy conversion or transfer discussed so far in this block, we have said that the objects involved and their surroundings become warmer, and this indicates that some of the energy is converted into internal energy. But why is this the case? What exactly is internal energy anyway, and how can the internal energy of an object be altered? In this section we will answer these questions. You will also have the opportunity to make some practical measurements relating to internal energy changes.

The practical work in Activity 6.1 may require some preparation, so we suggest you read the notes for this activity before you start this section.

6.1 What is internal energy?

As the name suggests, internal energy is stored *within* a substance, and to understand this we need to go back to the particle model of matter that was introduced in Block 2. According to this model, all molecules in a substance are in continual random motion. The motion of the molecules is different in solids, liquids and gases, but in all three states the molecules have a wide range of speeds, and their speeds are continually changing as the result of collisions and interactions. However, the mean speed associated with the random motion of the molecules is always related to the temperature.

How does the mean speed of random motion of the molecules in solids, liquids and gases change when the temperature increases, and how does the mean kinetic energy change?

You saw in Block 2, Section 6 that if the temperature increases, the mean speed of the molecules increases. The mean kinetic energy must increase too, since kinetic energy is proportional to the square of the speed.

So a higher temperature means that the molecules have greater kinetic energy. This *kinetic energy* associated with the random motion of molecules is one component of the internal energy of any object, and so when we raise an object's temperature, we increase its internal energy.

The other component of the internal energy of an object is associated with the *potential energy* of the molecules — stored energy that is associated with the forces that bind atoms together into molecules, and that bind molecules together in the solid and liquid states. We can explain the origin of this potential energy by using gravitational energy as an analogy. Earlier in this block, when we discussed the potential energy associated with the force of gravity, you saw that if you increased the separation of two objects that are attracted to each other by gravitational forces, then their gravitational (potential) energy increases. For example, there is a gravitational force between this book and the Earth: if you lift the book so that you increase the separation between the book and the Earth, then you increase the book's gravitational (potential) energy (Figure 6.1a).

The attractive force between two molecules is analogous to the gravitational force between the Earth and the book, though it is far stronger than the force of gravity. If the distance between two molecules is increased, then there is an increase in the potential energy associated with the forces between the molecules (Figure 6.1b). Within any object there are a huge number of molecules, and each of them will be attracted to all of its neighbours. So there will be a huge number of molecular

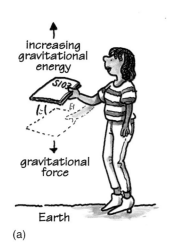

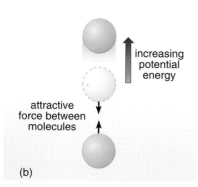

Figure 6.1 (a) The gravitational potential energy increases when the separation between a book and the Earth increases. (b) The potential energy of two molecules increases when the separation between them increases.

potential energies. These potential energies are the second important component of the internal energy of an object. So the total **internal energy** of an object is the *sum of kinetic and potential energies of all of the molecules* in the object.

We said earlier that when we increase the temperature of an object we increase the kinetic energy of the molecules, and this means that the internal energy of the object increases. But we can change the internal energy in other ways, and one way to do this is by changing the state of a substance, for example, by vaporizing a liquid. The separation of the molecules in a gas is generally far larger than in a liquid, so work has to be done on the molecules to increase their separation, and this leads to an increase in their *potential* energy. As a result, the internal energy of a gas at the boiling temperature is greater than the internal energy of the same mass of the liquid at the same temperature. The kinetic energy associated with the random motion of the molecules is essentially the same for the gas and for the liquid since they are at the same temperature, but the potential energy of the molecules in the gas is higher than the potential energy of the molecules in the liquid.

Another very important way to change the internal energy is by a chemical reaction, and this is rather different from changing the temperature or changing the state of a substance. In a chemical reaction, atoms swap partners, so the molecules produced in a chemical reaction are made up from different atoms linked in different ways from those in the reacting molecules. This means that the potential energy associated with forces between neighbouring atoms will be different. So a chemical reaction also leads to a change of internal energy. Earlier in this block we talked about changes in chemical energy when discussing the energy changes associated with a chemical reaction, and we will continue to do this. But you should bear in mind that **chemical energy** changes in a chemical reaction are really a particular type of internal energy change associated with the atoms and molecules of an object or substance.

6.1.1 Conversion of kinetic energy to internal energy

With this interpretation of internal energy, it is possible to explain why some of the kinetic energy of the locust in Activity 5.1 is converted into internal energy. As it moves through the air, the locust must displace molecules in the air from its path, and so there are a huge number of collisions between the molecules on the surface of the locust and molecules in the air. In fact, there are over 10^{23} collisions each second for each square centimetre of the locust's body! The net result of the collisions is that the molecules in the air bounce off the moving locust with slightly greater mean speed than they had before the collision, and the molecules of the locust will vibrate more vigorously than before. In both cases, the sum of the kinetic and potential energies associated with the random movements of the molecules increases, i.e. the internal energies of locust and air increase. And this exactly balances the decrease in the sum of the kinetic energy and the gravitational energy of the locust as a whole, so the total amount of energy is conserved.

This description is based on an analysis of the microscopic interactions between the molecules of the locust and the molecules of the surrounding air. We can describe the same situation in a different way by thinking about it on a larger scale. The huge number of molecular collisions constitute a force on the locust, which is usually described as being caused by air resistance. This force does work on the locust as it moves through the air, and it results in an increase in the internal energy of both the locust and the air, so both get warmer. The increases in internal energy exactly balance the decrease in the sum of the kinetic and gravitational energy of the locust as a whole.

It is important to distinguish between the two different types of kinetic energy that we have been discussing in this section. The locust *as a whole* has kinetic energy $\frac{1}{2}mv^2$, where m is the mass of the locust and v is its speed. But in addition to this, all of the molecules *within* the locust are vibrating randomly, whether the locust as a whole is moving or stationary, and it is the kinetic energy of these random vibrations that contributes to the internal energy of the locust.

The increase in internal energy of a moving locust caused by air resistance is really rather small and it would be very difficult to measure the associated, tiny change in temperature. For objects moving at higher speeds, the conversion of kinetic energy to internal energy may be much greater and the corresponding temperature rise much more dramatic (Figure 6.2).

Figure 6.2 The long streak of light is the trail of a meteor, a small extraterrestrial piece of rock probably no larger than a grain of sand. Meteors enter the Earth's atmosphere at speeds of up to $7 \times 10^4\,\mathrm{m\,s^{-1}}$, and their surfaces can be heated to over $2\,000\,°\mathrm{C}$ because of air resistance.

Air resistance and friction are always present to some extent on Earth and this means that kinetic energy is always being converted into internal energy. So moving objects always slow down and eventually stop, unless energy is continually supplied to keep them moving. This conversion from kinetic energy to internal energy is a one-way process though. It is impossible to convert the random kinetic energy associated with the internal energy of an object back into an orderly kinetic energy of the whole object.

6.1.2 Increasing the internal energy by heating

The internal energy of the locust or the meteor in the above examples increased because of the work done by the force caused by air resistance. However, this isn't the only way to increase the internal energy of an object. For example, when you make a cup of tea, you don't boil the water by beating it vigorously with a spoon or whirling the pan very rapidly through the air (or at least, most people don't). A more conventional way of bringing water to its boiling temperature is to place it in contact with an object at a higher temperature — for example, the heating element in an electric kettle. The fact that the heating element is at a higher temperature means that the mean kinetic energy of its molecules is greater than the mean kinetic energy of the surrounding water molecules. Collisions between water molecules and molecules of the heating element will, on average, result in water molecules rebounding faster than before and molecules of the heating element moving slower than before. This means that energy is transferred from the heating element to the water. Of course, while the kettle is switched on, electrical energy is continually converted into internal energy in the element, thus maintaining it at a higher temperature than the water. We will discuss this in more detail in Section 7.

This transfer of energy resulting from contact between objects at different temperatures is known as a transfer of heat*. In other words:

> **heat** is energy which flows from a higher temperature to a lower temperature because of the temperature difference, and when heat is transferred to an object, the internal energy of that object increases.

The internal energy of an object can therefore be increased either by supplying heat to it, or by doing work on it, or by some combination of the two.

6.2   Specific heat — relating heat transfer to temperature change

Having thought about what internal energy is and how it can be changed, we now consider how heat transfer affects the temperature of an object.

⬤   How do you think that the amount of heat transferred to an object might be related to the temperature rise that it produces?

◯   If you think that a larger amount of heat will produce a larger temperature rise, then you are correct. You may think that the heat transferred is *proportional* to the temperature rise, and that is an even better description of the relationship.

If we use the symbol q to represent the heat transferred, we can write:

$$q \propto \Delta T \tag{6.1}$$

where ΔT means the change in the temperature.

The internal energy of, say, a cupful of tea is the sum of the kinetic and potential energies of all of its constituent molecules. Obviously a second, identical cupful of tea will have the same internal energy as the first, and so both cupfuls together will have twice this amount of internal energy. Experimentally, we find that in order to raise the temperature of water by a particular amount ΔT, we have to transfer twice as much heat to 200 g of water as we do to 100 g. So, the heat q transferred to produce a temperature change of ΔT is also proportional to the mass m of an object:

$$q \propto m \times \Delta T \tag{6.2}$$

This proportionality relationship is illustrated in Figure 6.3.

* The word heat is often used incorrectly to mean internal energy, for example, in phrases like 'the kinetic energy was converted into heat' or 'the heat contained by an object'. You should remember that in a strict scientific sense, heat only refers to a *transfer* of energy caused by a difference in temperature.

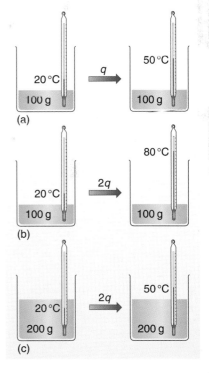

Figure 6.3   (a) If heat q is required to raise the temperature of 100 g of water from 20 °C to 50 °C, a temperature difference of 30 °C, then (b) $2q$ is required to raise the same mass through twice the temperature difference (60 °C), and (c) $2q$ is required to raise the temperature of twice the mass through the same temperature difference as in (a).

As before, this proportionality relationship can be turned into an equation by introducing a constant of proportionality, for which we will use the symbol c, so:

$$q = cm\Delta T \tag{6.3}$$

The constant of proportionality c is known as the specific heat (or in full as the specific heat capacity). Note that the symbol c that is conventionally used for specific heat is the same as that used for the speed of light. This is unlikely to lead to confusion because the two quantities rarely appear in the same context.

If Equation 6.3 is rearranged to make c the subject (by dividing both sides by $m\Delta T$), we can write:

$$c = \frac{q}{m\Delta T} \tag{6.4}$$

What is the appropriate unit of specific heat if heat (which has the same unit as energy) and mass are expressed in SI units and temperature in °C?

As always, the units on both sides of Equation 6.4 must balance. So

$$\text{unit of } c = \text{ unit of } \left(\frac{q}{m\Delta T}\right) = \frac{J}{kg \times °C} = J\,kg^{-1}\,°C^{-1}$$

Equation 6.4 can be expressed in words by saying that the **specific heat** is the amount of energy that has to be transferred to one unit of mass of material for one unit of temperature increase. Alternatively, we can say that the specific heat (in the unit quoted above) is the amount of energy in joules that has to be transferred to 1 kg of material to raise its temperature by 1 °C.

Different materials have very different values of specific heats, and these values also vary with temperature and pressure. The specific heats of some common materials are listed in Table 6.1. You will notice that no value is given for the specific heat of water. That is because we are going to ask you to measure it for yourself in Activity 6.1.

Table 6.1 Specific heats of some common materials at standard atmospheric pressure (1 013 millibar — see Block 2, Section 6.2) and 25 °C.

Substance	Specific heat /J kg^{-1} °C^{-1}
mercury	1.4×10^2
copper	3.8×10^2
glass	8.4×10^2
aluminium	9.0×10^2
air	1.0×10^3
paraffin	2.1×10^3
water	

Question 6.1 (a) How much energy is required to heat a copper pan, mass 0.50 kg, from 20 °C to 100 °C? (You will need to use information from Table 6.1.)

(b) *Estimate* how much energy would be required to heat (i) a 250 g copper pan, (ii) a 0.50 kg aluminium pan, through the same temperature difference as in part (a). ◀

Activity 6.1 Measuring the specific heat of water

This activity will give you an opportunity to develop a variety of practical work skills in the context of measuring an important property of water. ◀

6.3 The absolute scale of temperature

We have said that the mean kinetic energy of the constituent molecules of an object increases when the temperature of the object increases. It follows that, as an object cools, so the mean kinetic energy of the molecules decreases. Eventually a point is reached at which the molecules have a minimum kinetic energy, and no further cooling can be achieved. The temperature at which this occurs is known as **absolute zero**, and this is the lowest temperature possible. On the Celsius scale, this temperature has a value of −273.15 °C.

For many scientific purposes, it makes sense to define a temperature scale for which zero on the scale corresponds to this absolute zero of temperature, and on such a scale negative temperatures are impossible. The scale with this property, that is widely used by scientists, is known as the **absolute temperature scale**; it is also known as the Kelvin scale, named after the British physicist and engineer William Thomson, Lord Kelvin (1824–1907). The unit of temperature on this scale is called the **kelvin**, symbol K, and this is the SI unit of temperature. A kelvin is the same size as the Celsius degree, so there are 100 kelvin between the normal freezing and boiling temperatures of water. The absolute and Celsius scales are compared in Figure 6.4. To convert degrees Celsius into kelvin, you just add 273.15 to the Celsius temperature. Thus the normal freezing temperature of water (0 °C) is 273.15 kelvin, or 273.15 K.

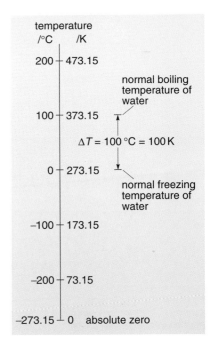

Figure 6.4 A comparison of the Celsius (°C) and absolute (K) temperature scales.

⬤ What is the value in kelvin of the Earth's mean surface temperature, 15 °C?

◯ 15 °C is (15 + 273.15) K, or about 288 K. (Note that we've quoted the absolute temperature to the nearest degree because the Celsius temperature was quoted to that precision.)

The convention for the absolute scale is that the temperature is written without a degree symbol, and so 300 K is read as 'three hundred kelvin' and *not* 'three hundred *degrees* kelvin'.

We have stressed in this block the importance of using SI units in calculations, so you may be wondering why we have used degrees Celsius until now. The answer is that in all our calculations so far we have been concerned with *changes* of temperature; for example, you calculated the energy required to heat a pan through 80 °C — a temperature *change* of 80 °C. The size of a kelvin is exactly the same as the size of a °C, so temperature differences have the same numerical value on both scales. In SI units we should quote the specific heat of water as $4.2 \times 10^3 \, \text{J kg}^{-1} \, \text{K}^{-1}$, rather than $4.2 \times 10^3 \, \text{J kg}^{-1} \, °\text{C}^{-1}$. We have chosen to use the more familiar unit here, rather than convert between °C and K all the time. However, there are situations where it is important to use the absolute temperature in calculations, and you will meet an example in Section 8.2.

Question 6.2 Write down equations for converting (a) temperature in degrees Celsius into temperature in kelvin, and (b) temperature in kelvin into temperature in degrees Celsius. ◀

6.4 Latent heat of vaporization

Energy must be supplied to raise the temperature of a substance, but as you know from Blocks 1 and 2, energy must also be supplied to change the *state* of a substance. Thus, when you heat water in an electric kettle, its temperature increases until it boils at about 100 °C. At this point, the temperature stops rising, and the energy transferred to the water from the heating element now transforms liquid water into water vapour.

⬤ In Section 6.1, we explained why energy has to be supplied to convert a liquid into a gas. Try to recall this explanation without referring back to the earlier section.

You can check your explanation by rereading the penultimate paragraph of Section 6.1 on page p. 37.

In the spirit of the more quantitative approach of this block, we now ask *how much* energy does it take to change a liquid into a gas?

Applying the same reasoning as we did when discussing specific heat, we can assume that the energy required — that is, the amount of heat transferred — is proportional to the mass of liquid converted into gas. We can express this as:

$$q \propto m \tag{6.5}$$

In this case the temperature does not change and so we do not have to consider it. This simple proportionality relationship can now be converted into an equation in the usual way by introducing a constant of proportionality, which we will call L:

$$q = Lm \tag{6.6}$$

The constant of proportionality L is known as the **latent heat of vaporization**, and we can define it as the energy required to vaporize one unit of mass of the liquid at its boiling temperature.

What is the SI unit of the latent heat of vaporization?

If we divide both sides of Equation 6.6 by m to make L the subject, we obtain

$L = \dfrac{q}{m}$. The units of both sides of this equation must be the same, so:

$$\text{unit of } L = \text{unit of } \left(\frac{q}{m}\right) = \frac{\text{J}}{\text{kg}} = \text{J kg}^{-1}$$

As with specific heat, the value of the latent heat of vaporization is different for different materials. Table 6.2 lists values for some common materials, which have boiling temperatures ranging from $-183\,°\text{C}$ for oxygen to $2\,567\,°\text{C}$ for copper. You will be able to write in the value of the latent heat of vaporization of water after you have completed Activity 6.2.

Table 6.2 Latent heat of vaporization of some common materials at standard atmospheric pressure.

Substance	Latent heat/J kg^{-1}
oxygen	2.1×10^5
mercury	2.9×10^5
water	
copper	5.2×10^6
aluminium	1.1×10^7

Question 6.3 In Victorian winters, mulled ale was often made by plunging a red-hot poker into a tankard of ale at room temperature, which resulted in some of the ale boiling off as steam (water vapour) and the ale warming up. The poker was metal, and the ale consisted mainly of water molecules. Describe what happened to the water molecules and to the atoms in the poker during this process. ◀

Question 6.4 Liquid oxygen boils at $-183\,°\text{C}$ at standard atmospheric pressure. It can be stored for short periods in a thermos flask, but the heat transferred to the flask from the warmer surroundings causes the liquid oxygen to boil.

(a) What is the boiling temperature of liquid oxygen on the absolute temperature scale?

(b) If $9.5 \times 10^4\,\text{J}$ of heat is transferred to the flask in an hour, what mass of liquid oxygen is converted into gas in this period? ◀

Activity 6.2 *Measuring the latent heat of vaporization of water*

In this activity you will use data for the mass of water vaporized from a kettle of boiling water in a known time to determine the latent heat of vaporization of water. ◀

6.4.1 Latent heat and the Earth's surface temperature

As an example of a practical application of the idea of latent heat, we return to the Earth's water cycle, which was introduced in Block 1 and discussed in more detail in Block 2. You should recall that the continual cycling of water between the Earth's surface and the atmosphere plays a significant part in controlling the global mean surface temperature (GMST). The two most important aspects of the water cycle in terms of heat transfer are the evaporation of liquid water at the Earth's surface and the condensation of water vapour in the atmosphere to form clouds. The net result of these two processes is a transfer of energy: from internal energy of the Earth's surface, via latent heat into internal energy of water vapour, and then to internal energy of the gases in the atmosphere when the water vapour condenses. The result is that the temperature of the Earth's surface decreases and the temperature of the atmosphere increases. This is illustrated in Figure 6.5.

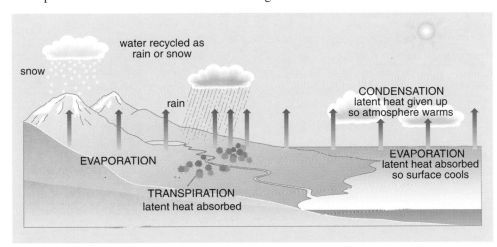

Figure 6.5 The water cycle transfers energy from the Earth's surface to the atmosphere.

Armed with your new found value of the latent heat of vaporization of water (Activity 6.2), you are now in a position to calculate the rate at which energy is transported into the atmosphere by latent heat.

The first step in this calculation is to relate the energy the Earth loses when water evaporates from its surface to the mass of water evaporated, and we can do that by using Equation 6.6. Consider a period of one year, and assume that a mass m of water evaporates from the whole of the Earth's surface during this period. The total energy q required to evaporate the water in this one-year period is given by $q = Lm$. We know the value of the latent heat of vaporization L of water, but what is the mass of water evaporated in a year?

Here we have to be rather subtle. Since mean sea-level around the world varies very little from one year to the next, the total evaporation from the Earth's surface in any one year must be balanced by the total precipitation. (Here the term 'evaporation' includes *all* water evaporated from land and sea surfaces and water transpired by plants.) So although it is rather difficult to measure the amount evaporated directly, we can assume it is equal to the mean annual precipitation. Now in Block 2, Section 7.1, the depth of precipitation averaged over the Earth's surface per year was given as about 1 000 mm, and we calculated that the mass of this amount of water is 5.1×10^{17} kg. So the mass of the water that evaporates from the Earth's surface each year must also be 5.1×10^{17} kg.

Question 6.5   What is the energy required to evaporate 5.1×10^{17} kg of water from the Earth's surface? (Assume that the latent heat of vaporization of water is 2.6×10^6 J kg^{-1}.) ◄

The value you calculated in Question 6.5 is the annual energy requirement for evaporating water from the Earth's surface. This energy is about a quarter of the energy of the solar electromagnetic radiation that reaches the top of the Earth's atmosphere in a year.

The cooling effect of the water cycle therefore has a very significant effect on the Earth's surface temperature. In fact, if this evaporative cooling of the surface were to disappear (but everything else were to remain the same), the Earth's GMST would rise by more than 10 °C.

6.5   Summary of Section 6

The internal energy of an object is the sum of the kinetic energy associated with random motion of the molecules in the object and the potential energy associated with the attractive forces between the atoms and molecules. The internal energy can be increased by supplying heat to an object (that is by transferring energy by means of a temperature difference) or by doing work on an object (for example by forces associated with friction or air resistance).

The heat transferred to an object of mass m and specific heat c to produce temperature change ΔT is $q = cm\Delta T$. The specific heat of a material is equal to the heat transferred to one unit of mass to produce one unit of temperature change;

$$c = \frac{q}{m\Delta T}.$$

On the absolute, or Kelvin, temperature scale, 0 K corresponds to the lowest temperature possible, and is called absolute zero. The temperature in kelvin is found by adding 273.15 to the value of the temperature in °C.

The latent heat of vaporization L of a liquid is the energy required to convert one unit of mass of the liquid into the vapour; $L = \dfrac{q}{m}$. The latent heat associated with evaporation and condensation of water transfers energy from the Earth's surface to the atmosphere, with the consequence that the Earth's GMST is significantly lower than it would be in the absence of this process.

Activity 3.2   Keeping track of symbols and equations (continued)
This is an appropriate point to check that you have included the symbols, equations and units from the last few sections in your glossary. ◄

Electrical energy

7

In Activity 6.1, you converted electrical energy into internal energy of water in a kettle, and indeed you almost certainly convert electrical energy into other forms of energy every day of your life. Electricity has revolutionized life all over the world and it is probably true to say that the harnessing of electrical energy is the single most important technological advance of the last two centuries. Not only can it be used to provide light, heat and kinetic energy on a vast scale, but it is also the subtle energy source which drives all electronic devices. There are two reasons for the extra-ordinary utility of electricity. First, electrical energy can be transported over vast distances at little cost; second, and more importantly, it can be transformed into many other forms of energy very easily.

○ Think for a few minutes about uses of electricity in your home. List some of the different forms of energy into which electrical energy is converted.

○ Your answer might have included some of the following forms of energy, though we wouldn't expect you to think of them all — and you may have thought of some that aren't included:

- electromagnetic radiation — light from a light bulb or television, microwave radiation in a microwave oven, ultraviolet radiation from a sunlamp, infrared radiation from the heating element of a grill or from the remote control device for a television;

- kinetic energy of any appliance that has a motor, pump or fan;

- gravitational energy from a lift or hoist;

- sound energy from a hi-fi or television, or from any 'noisy' appliance with moving parts;

- internal energy in any appliance that gets hot, such as a cooker, kettle, washing machine or tumble-drier, light bulb, etc.

In order to appreciate fully the nature of electrical energy, we first need to make a short detour to introduce some of the basic concepts of electricity, including electric charge, current and voltage. We will then be able to discuss how the amounts of electrical energy associated with various processes can be calculated and measured.

7.1 Electric charge

The Ancient Greeks made observations on what we would now call electrical phenomena and recorded the fact that when a piece of amber is rubbed with silk it will attract small, light objects. Indeed, our word *electricity* comes from the Greek *electron* meaning amber. Other examples of natural electricity abound. For example, after vigorously brushing your hair with a plastic hairbrush, you may have noticed that strands of hair are attracted to the brush, particularly if you have fine hair (Figure 7.1).

○ Spend a few minutes thinking of other examples of the effects of naturally produced electricity.

Figure 7.1 An example of electrical attraction.

○ You might have thought of dust being attracted to records; crackles (which are the sound produced by small sparks) when you remove clothes made from synthetic fibres on a dry day and also these clothes making the hairs on your skin stand on end; balloons sticking to the wall after being rubbed on your clothing; and, of course, the most dramatic example of all, lightning. Electricity is also involved in the control of all muscular and nervous activity in the body — including making your heart beat. Even the thoughts you have as you read these words are associated with electrical activity in your brain.

We can explain these and many other phenomena with a simple model that has been developed from ideas first put forward by the American scientist and statesman Benjamin Franklin (1707–1790). According to this model:

- electrical phenomena are caused by a property of matter called **electric charge**, or charge for short;
- there are two kinds of electric charge, called positive charge and negative charge;
- like charges (with the same sign) repel one another; unlike charges (with opposite signs) attract one another (Figure 7.2);
- all matter contains an enormous number of electrically charged particles, with approximately equal numbers of positively charged particles and negatively charged particles. Objects with equal quantities of both types of charge are designated electrically neutral.
- certain actions, such as vigorous rubbing, can transfer charged particles between two initially neutral objects, causing one to become positively charged and the other negatively charged.

We can use this model to explain qualitatively why the hairbrush and hair (in Figure 7.1) attract each other. The brushing motion causes a transfer of charge between the hair and the brush leaving one positively charged and the other negatively charged. The two unlike charges attract one another, causing the hair to move towards the brush. In the language of science, we can say that the unlike charges exert attractive forces on each other. For obvious reasons, the force that occurs between charges is called an **electric force**.

The unit of charge in the SI system is called the **coulomb** (symbol C). This is rather a large unit compared to the amount of electric charge on a hairbrush after hair-brushing, which might be about 10^{-8} C. However, if we had two objects that each had a charge of 1 C and they were separated by 1 m, then the force between them would be about 10^{10} N — that's about 10^4 times greater than the force produced by the engines of a jumbo jet during take off!

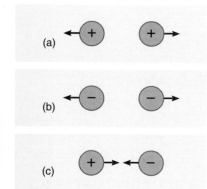

Figure 7.2 (a) and (b) Repulsive forces between objects with like charges, and (c) attractive forces between objects with unlike charges.

7.2 Conductors and insulators

We can take our understanding of electricity a little further by considering Benjamin Franklin's simple model of positive and negative charges in the light of 20th century ideas about the atom. As you have learned already in Block 2, all matter consists of atoms. We will say a lot more about the structure of atoms in Blocks 6 and 7, but for now it is enough to know that within every atom there is a tiny *nucleus* surrounded by a number of even smaller particles called **electrons**. The electrons each carry a negative charge and the nucleus is positively charged. The reason the nucleus and electrons of an atom stay together is precisely the same as the reason your hair is attracted to a hairbrush — the electric force pulls them together.

All electrons have the same charge, which is very small, -1.6×10^{-19} C. The charge on the atomic nucleus is equal in magnitude but opposite in sign to the total charge of all the electrons in an atom. Thus atoms are electrically neutral overall.

Question 7.1 There are roughly 10^{26} electrons in each kilogram of the human body. Estimate the total negative charge and the total positive charge in your body in coulombs. ◄

Question 7.2 At the end of Section 7.1 we quoted the magnitude of the force between two objects that each have a charge of 1 C and that are separated by 1 m. The answer to Question 7.1 showed that the positive charge content of your body and the negative charge content are each far greater than 1 C. In view of this, how can you sit in the same room as another human being (who will contain similar amounts of charge) without literally blowing each other away? ◄

Atoms can lose or gain electrons to leave themselves with a net positive or negative charge, and they are then called *ions*. From the point of view of electricity, we can classify substances into two kinds: *electrical insulators*, in which electrons and ions are not able to move freely through the substance, and *electrical conductors*, in which electrons or ions can move freely. Examples of electrical insulators are rubber, glass and most kinds of plastic, and examples of electrical conductors are metals and salty water. The difference between these two types of materials is vital for the distribution of electricity and for the operation of the electrical appliances in your home (Figure 7.3).

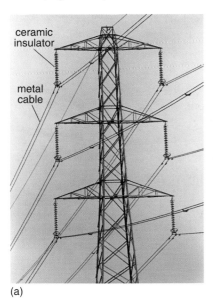

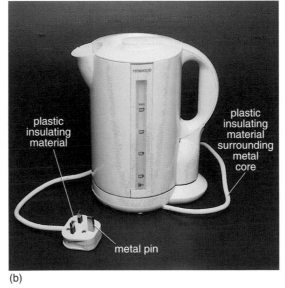

(a)   (b)

Figure 7.3 (a) Electrons can move freely through the metal cables used to distribute electricity but not through the ceramic insulators used to support the cables. (b) Metal pins in the plug and the metal core in the cable conduct electricity to appliances, whilst plastic insulation prevents the electricity from flowing through people (who can be regarded as bags of conducting salty water).

There is a third class of materials, called semiconductors, which have become tremendously important over the last 50 years as the basis of the electronics and computing industries, but there is not space to deal with their properties in this course.

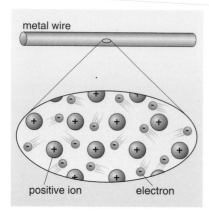

metal wire

positive ion   electron

Figure 7.4 A fixed array of positively charged ions and a 'gas' of negatively charged electrons in an electrically conducting solid. The positive charges on the ions and the negative charges on the electrons balance, so the solid is electrically neutral.

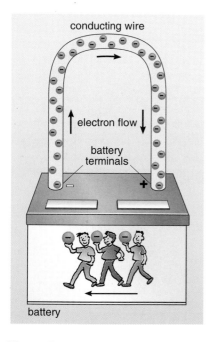

conducting wire

electron flow

battery terminals

battery

Figure 7.6 A battery can maintain a continuous flow of electrons from its negative terminal to its positive terminal through a conducting wire. At the same time there is a net flow of negative charge within the battery from the positive terminal to the negative terminal. The arrows show the direction of negative charge flow.

7.3 Electric current

In a conducting solid, such as a metal, electrons can move around fairly freely, rather like the molecules in a gas. Therefore we can picture such a solid as consisting of a 'gas' of negatively charged electrons moving randomly through a fixed array of positively charged ions, as shown in Figure 7.4. (Think back to the description of the arrangement of particles in a solid given in Block 2, Section 6.1.)

Now let's consider what would happen if we transferred all the electrons from one end of a conducting wire to the other. There would then be a large excess of positive charge at the end from which the negatively charged electrons had been removed, and a large excess of negative charge at the other end, as shown in Figure 7.5. The electrons, which are free to move, would rush back towards the positively charged end of the wire under the action of the electric force, until their negative charges once

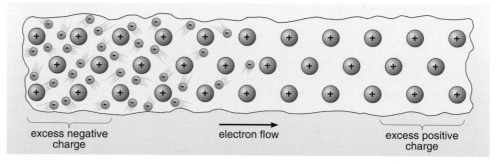

excess negative charge   electron flow   excess positive charge

Figure 7.5 Electrons migrating in a conducting wire under the action of electric forces due to the charge imbalance at the ends. The arrow shows the direction of movement of the electrons.

again just balanced the positive charges. This flow of negatively charged electrons constitutes what we call an **electric current** (or current for short) in the wire. In this case the electric current would peter out very quickly, as soon as the electrons had redistributed themselves to cancel out the charge imbalance.

If we wanted to keep an electric current flowing through the wire, we would need to continually remove electrons from the 'positive end' and replace them at the 'negative end'. In this way a steady state would be reached, and the electrons would keep travelling along the wire attracted by the positive charge. This is exactly what an electric battery does. When a conducting wire is connected between the positive and negative terminals of a battery, one end of the wire becomes positively charged and the other negatively charged. The electric force causes electrons to move through the wire towards the positive terminal of the battery, where they are removed from the wire, and at the same time the negative terminal supplies more electrons to the wire. Within the battery there is a net flow of negative charge from the positive terminal to the negative terminal, which balances the flow through the wire, so the charges don't continually build up at the battery terminals (Figure 7.6). The energy required to drive this process comes from chemical reactions that take place within the battery.

Now when we think about the operation of an electrical device, we don't usually consider the number of electrons, or the quantity of charge, that flows through it. Instead we consider the electric current, which is the *rate* at which charge flows through the device. Electric current is defined as the quantity of charge passing a given point in unit time, so:

$$\text{current} = \frac{\text{charge}}{\text{time}}$$

If we represent the electric current by the symbol I, and electric charge by Q, then we can rewrite this word equation as:

$$I = \frac{Q}{t} \tag{7.1}$$

The SI unit of current is the **ampere** (often shortened to amp, symbol A). A current of one ampere corresponds to a flow of one coulomb of charge per second:

$$1\,\text{A} = \frac{1\,\text{C}}{1\,\text{s}} = 1\,\text{C s}^{-1} \tag{7.2}$$

You will probably have come across this unit in the specification of electric cables or fuses: a 5 A cable can safely carry a current of 5 A, or $5\,\text{C s}^{-1}$, and a 13 A fuse will blow when the current exceeds 13 A.

7.4 Electrical energy and voltage

When we discussed motion under gravity (Section 4.2), it was useful to think about the situation in terms of changes in gravitational potential energy, which we shortened to gravitational energy. In a similar way, the motion of electrons in an electric current can be explained by considering changes in their electrical potential energy, and we will generally abbreviate this to electrical energy.

To see how this works, consider first the flow of water between the two tanks illustrated in Figure 7.7a. Tank A is initially filled to a higher level than tank B. If the valve in the pipe is opened, water will flow through the pipe. This is analogous to the flow of electrons through a conductor from the negatively charged end to the positively charged end, as discussed in the last section. The flow of water in the pipe will slow down and eventually stop when the levels in the tanks equalize, again analogous to the electrical situation. If we want to maintain a steady flow of water in the pipe, we need to transport water from tank B back to tank A to maintain a difference between the water levels, and this can be done with a pump (Figure 7.7b). This is analogous to the action of the battery.

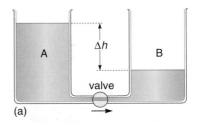

Let's now consider the energy changes in these two situations. From the discussion in Section 4.2, when water flows from tank A to tank B, its gravitational energy decreases.

● What is the decrease in the gravitational energy of a mass m of water that falls through a height Δh, as in Figure 7.7?

○ The decrease in gravitational energy is given by:

$$\Delta E_\text{g} = mg\Delta h \tag{4.8}$$

The gravitational energy is initially converted into kinetic energy of the water as it flows through the pipe and into tank B, but this kinetic energy is eventually converted into internal energy because of friction between the water and the pipe, so the water gets warmer.

You might guess that a similar argument applies to the electrons in the wire — and you would be correct. We can think of electrical energy associated with the electric

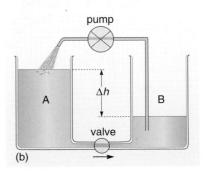

Figure 7.7   (a) If the valve is open, water will flow from tank A to tank B until the water levels become equal. (b) A steady flow of water from tank A to tank B can be maintained by using a pump to circulate water back from B to A.

49

force, in the same way as we think of gravitational energy associated with the force of gravity. When the electrons flow through the wire, their electrical energy decreases, and this energy is initially converted into kinetic energy. However, the moving electrons undergo frequent collisions with the positive ions, causing them to vibrate more vigorously and thus transforming some of the kinetic energy of the electrons to internal energy of the wire, which therefore heats up.

We can write down a very similar equation to Equation 4.8 to describe this change in electrical energy, which we represent by the symbol ΔE_e. In the gravitational case, the change in gravitational energy is proportional to the mass of the object which moves from one place to another. The change in electrical energy, however, is proportional to the electric charge Q that moves. Bearing in mind that gravitational forces act on objects with mass, and electric forces act on objects with charge, then this should seem reasonable. So we can write:

$$\Delta E_e \propto Q \qquad \text{or} \qquad \Delta E_e = \text{constant} \times Q \tag{7.3}$$

This proportionality probably also seems reasonable — if twice as much charge flows we would expect the change in electrical energy to be twice as great. The constant of proportionality in this relationship is a quantity known as the **voltage difference** of the battery, which we will represent by the symbol ΔV. The SI unit of voltage difference is the **volt**, abbreviated to V.

Thus the equation for the change in **electrical energy** when a charge Q moves through a voltage difference ΔV is:

$$\Delta E_e = Q\Delta V \tag{7.4}$$

If we use SI units for each of the three quantities in this equation then we see that $1\,\text{J} = 1\,\text{C} \times 1\,\text{V} = 1\,\text{C V}$.

Voltage difference is often referred to simply as *voltage*, and this is a term you are almost certainly familiar with. The value of the voltage is given on all batteries and electricity supplies. When someone talks of a 12 volt car battery, they mean that there is a voltage difference of 12 volts between the battery terminals.

Question 7.3   Calculate the change in electrical energy if a charge of 2 C flows through a conducting wire when its ends are connected to the terminals of a 12 V battery. ◀

7.5   Electric power

When an electric current flows through a conductor, electrical energy is continuously converted into other forms of energy, such as internal energy in a heating element, light from the filament of a bulb, or sound from a loudspeaker. In Section 3.3, we defined the rate at which energy is converted as the power. Once again, this is a concept that will be familiar to you in dealing with electrical appliances. Each of your appliances should have a power rating which tells you how rapidly the conversion from electrical energy to other forms of energy occurs. But how is the power rating related to current and voltage?

Electric power is the change in electrical energy per unit time, that is:

$$P = \frac{\Delta E_e}{t} \tag{7.5}$$

But we showed in Equation 7.4 that electrical energy is given by $\Delta E_e = Q\Delta V$, so if we substitute $Q\Delta V$ in place of ΔE_e we find:

$$P = \frac{Q\Delta V}{t} \tag{7.6}$$

Now remember that current is defined by $I = \dfrac{Q}{t}$ (Equation 7.1), so we can replace $\dfrac{Q}{t}$ in Equation 7.6 by I to obtain the equation:

$$P = I\Delta V \tag{7.7}$$

This relationship is very useful. Given any two of the quantities in Equation 7.7, we can calculate the remaining one. For example, suppose that a current of 2 A flows through a torch bulb connected to a 6 V battery. Then the power is given by:

$$P = I\Delta V = 2\,\text{A} \times 6\,\text{V} = 12\,\text{A V} = 12\,\text{W}$$

⬤ Use the definitions of the amp and the volt to confirm that 1 A V = 1 W.

○ 1 A = 1 C s⁻¹ (Equation 7.2), and 1 V = 1 J C⁻¹ (from Equation 7.4), so
1 A V = (1 C s⁻¹) × (1 J C⁻¹) = 1 J s⁻¹ = 1 W.

Question 7.4   An electric kettle operates from the 240 V mains electricity supply. The electric current through the heating element is 8.4 A. What is the power rating of the kettle element? ◀

Question 7.5   (a) Calculate the current flowing through a 20 W car headlamp bulb, which operates from a 12 V battery.

(b) What charge flows through the bulb in one minute? ◀

7.6   Summary of Section 7

There are two types of electric charge, positive and negative. Charged objects with the same sign repel each other, whereas those with opposite signs attract each other. An object is neutral if it contains equal amounts of positive and negative charge. The SI unit of charge is the coulomb, C.

Electrons are free to move in an electrical conductor. The flow of electrons constitutes an electric current, which is defined as flow of charge per unit time, $I = \dfrac{Q}{t}$. The SI unit of current is the amp; 1 A = 1 C s⁻¹.

The change in electrical energy when charge Q flows through a voltage difference ΔV is $\Delta E_e = Q\Delta V$. The SI unit of voltage difference is the volt, V.

Electrical power is the rate at which electrical energy is converted into other forms of energy; $P = \dfrac{\Delta E_e}{t} = I\Delta V$.

8 Energy from the Sun

In Section 5 we pointed out that the kinetic energy of a jumping locust was converted from chemical energy stored within the locust, and this in turn came from the chemical energy stored in the food eaten by the locust. If we go one step further back and ask 'Where does the energy stored in the food come from?' the answer is 'From the Sun'.

As we discussed in Block 4, in the process of photosynthesis solar energy is absorbed within chloroplasts in leaf cells of plants. Of course, the absorbed energy doesn't just raise the temperature of the cell. It also enables carbon dioxide to undergo a chemical reaction with water to produce glucose. So part of the energy absorbed is stored in the glucose as chemical energy. Eventually the glucose molecules are broken down into other molecules in the respiration process, and this may happen in other cells of the same plant, or in the cells of animals that eat plants. The chemical energy stored in the glucose is then released, and it enables other metabolic processes to take place within living cells. In a very real sense, the Sun is the source of all life on Earth.

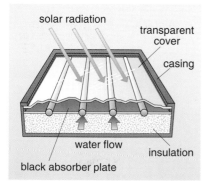

Figure 8.1 A solar collector on a house.

Figure 8.2 Diagram of a solar collector.

8.1 Uses of solar energy

As well as being the energy source for almost all life on Earth, solar energy can also be harnessed in a number of ways, both directly and indirectly, for a wide variety of uses.

Indirect use of solar energy occurs every time you burn a piece of wood. When a tree is alive, it absorbs solar energy through the leaves and converts this energy into chemical energy, which is stored within its cells. When you burn a piece of wood, the stored chemical energy is released, and is transferred to the surroundings in the form of heat and light, so that ultimately the internal energy in the immediate surroundings increases. The same is true of coal, natural gas, oil and oil-derived products, such as petrol. All were formed from the remains of life-forms which existed hundreds of millions of years ago. The next time you are driving your car, it is worth reflecting that you are using energy which originally came from the Sun long before humans existed on the Earth!

Question 8.1 As well as being the energy source for all of these fuels, solar energy is indirectly responsible for a number of so-called *renewable* energy sources. Can you name two, and explain the role that solar energy plays in each case? ◀

Many devices exist that convert solar radiation *directly* into other forms of energy. For example, solar collectors for domestic water heating are now commonplace (Figure 8.1), and Figure 8.2 shows how such a typical solar collector works. The incoming radiation is absorbed by the black metal plate, raising its temperature and raising the temperature of water in pipes attached to the plate. The heated water circulates from the collector to the hot-water tank in the house, where it transfers energy to the water stored in the tank, and then returns to the collector to be reheated.

⦿ The solar collectors shown in Figures 8.1 and 8.2 have a transparent plastic or glass sheet covering them. In terms of energy transfer, what is the main purpose of the covering sheet?

It creates a mini-greenhouse (Block 2, Box 5.2). There are two aspects to this. First, the solar electromagnetic radiation passes through the covering sheet, but the (longwave infrared) radiation emitted by the heated pipes and the backing plate is not transmitted and so the energy carried by this radiation is trapped within the device. Second, and more important, the covering sheet prevents heat escaping via convection.

The solar *collectors* shown in Figures 8.1 and 8.2 convert the energy of electromagnetic radiation into internal energy. In contrast, solar *cells* convert electromagnetic radiation directly into electrical energy. Solar cells are used to provide electrical power for a range of applications, from the instruments on Earth-orbiting satellites (Figure 8.3) to solar-powered calculators and watches.

8.2   The Earth's GMST — a final calculation

The Earth is a giant solar collector but, as you saw in Block 2, its atmosphere plays an essential role in raising the temperature of the Earth to a level at which life can exist. Without the atmosphere, the GMST would be below 0 °C, as we will show in this section.

In Block 2, the leaky tank was used as an analogy for how the Earth's surface reaches a steady state in which the incoming energy is balanced by the outgoing energy. The outgoing energy depends on the Earth's surface temperature, and so this temperature increases or decreases until the outgoing energy balances the incoming energy. In order to estimate the warming effect of the Earth's atmosphere, we need to do a calculation to see what the steady-state temperature would be if there were no atmosphere at all. The difference between the calculated temperature and the measured temperature must then be caused by the presence of the atmosphere. Fortunately, the calculation of the temperature when there is no atmosphere is quite straightforward, because in this situation we only have to consider outgoing energy due to electromagnetic radiation emitted from the Earth's surface, as shown in Figure 8.4. There will, of course, be no convection or latent heat transfer, and no absorption by, or emission from, the absent atmosphere.

Now the rate at which electromagnetic radiation is emitted by an object increases with increasing temperature. In order to do our calculation, we need to make this relationship more quantitative. Experiments show that the rate at which energy is emitted by an object is very sensitive to its temperature. In fact in many situations (including the one that interests us here) the power P of the radiation emitted from an object with area A at an absolute temperature T (in kelvin) is:

$$P = \sigma A T^4 \tag{8.1}$$

where σ, the Greek lower case letter sigma, is a constant of proportionality which has the value $5.67 \times 10^{-8} \, \text{W m}^{-2} \, \text{K}^{-4}$.

Question 8.2   Show that the units on the two sides of Equation 8.1 balance if P, A and T are in SI units. ◄

Now let's apply Equation 8.1 to emission from the Earth's surface. P is then the power of the radiation emitted by the Earth's surface, of area A, when its absolute temperature is T. In the absence of an atmosphere, in the steady state, this power must be equal to the rate at which the Earth absorbs solar radiation. But if there is no atmosphere, and therefore no clouds or aerosols either, then there is nothing to absorb

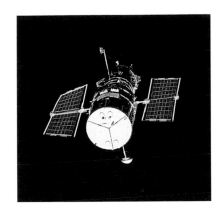

Figure 8.3   Solar cells on the Hubble Space Telescope. Each of the two panels is 11.8 m × 2.3 m, and they supply over 2.5 kW of electrical power in total.

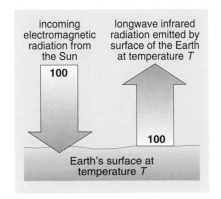

incoming electromagnetic radiation from the Sun

100

longwave infrared radiation emitted by surface of the Earth at temperature T

100

Earth's surface at temperature T

Figure 8.4   With no atmosphere, there would be an energy balance between electromagnetic radiation from the Sun absorbed by the Earth's surface and longwave infrared radiation emitted by the Earth's surface.

or scatter radiation before it reaches the Earth's surface. This means that all of the 1.74×10^{17} W of solar electromagnetic radiation intercepted by the Earth reaches its surface. About 85% of this radiation would be absorbed by the surface (assuming that the surface remains the same when the atmosphere is removed), and the remaining 15% would be reflected back to space.

Question 8.3 (a) What would be the rate at which solar energy was absorbed by the Earth's surface if there were no atmosphere? Express your answer in watts.

(b) What would be the rate (in watts) at which infrared radiation was emitted in the steady state?

(c) Show that, if the GMST were $-6\,°C$ in the absence of an atmosphere, the power of the radiation emitted by the Earth's surface would balance the solar electromagnetic radiation absorbed, so that the Earth's surface would be in a steady state. (The area A of the Earth's surface is $5.1 \times 10^{14}\,m^2$.) ◀

As Question 8.3 shows, the Earth's GMST would be inhospitably frigid in the absence of the atmosphere. This indicates that the atmosphere is not only vital for providing the oxygen essential for animal life and carbon dioxide essential for plant life, but it is also vital for raising the GMST to levels that make life possible.

8.3 Nuclear fusion — energy from the heart of the Sun

In the last section, we followed the energy trail back to the Sun, which is the source of much of the energy that is available on the Earth. If we take the next logical step and ask where solar energy comes from, the answer is that the Sun is a vast nuclear power station, and the ultimate source of solar energy is the nuclear reactions in the Sun itself (see the photos on title page).

Earlier in the course, we discussed briefly the nuclear fusion process that occurs in the Sun's core (Block 3, Section 5.1.1). In this process, the principal constituent of the Sun, hydrogen, is converted into helium. Now a characteristic of a nuclear fusion reaction like this is that the total mass of the products of the reaction — mainly helium — is *less* than the mass of the reacting hydrogen. Mass seems to disappear. Yet vast quantities of energy are produced, seemingly from nowhere.

The key to understanding what is going on in the Sun, and in other nuclear reactions, lies in Einstein's famous equation:

$$E = mc^2 \tag{8.2}$$

According to Einstein's theory of relativity, energy and mass are not distinct quantities. Energy can be transformed into mass, and mass can be transformed into energy, just as kinetic energy can be transferred into gravitational energy, and vice versa. Thus mass is a form of energy. Equation 8.2 tells us the conversion factor from mass to energy: the amount of energy E that is contained in mass m is mc^2, where c is the speed of light ($3.0 \times 10^8\,m\,s^{-1}$). This is a difficult concept to grasp, so let's look at some consequences to clarify exactly what it means.

○ According to Einstein's equation, how much energy is contained in 1 kg of matter?

○ $E = mc^2 = 1 \text{ kg} \times (3.0 \times 10^8 \text{ m s}^{-1})^2 = 9 \times 10^{16} \text{ kg m}^2 \text{ s}^{-2} = 9 \times 10^{16} \text{ J}$.

This is a huge amount of energy. It is equivalent to the energy produced by a 300 MW power station operating for about 10 years, or alternatively, it is enough to keep a 100 W light bulb operating for about 30 million years! So a small amount of matter is equivalent to a very large amount of energy. It is the release of some of the energy that is stored in matter that is responsible for the large outputs of energy from fusion reactions in the Sun and from the nuclear reactions in a nuclear power station. The same conversion of matter into energy, occurring in an uncontrolled fashion, is responsible for devastating weapons of war.

Now let's look at the conversion the other way round. Consider what happens when we heat one kilogram (one litre) of water from 0 °C to 100 °C. The energy supplied to the water can be calculated from Equation 6.3, $q = cm\Delta T$, and it is $4.2 \times 10^5 \text{ J}$ (don't forget that the c in this equation represents specific heat). So the energy of one litre of water at 100 °C is greater by $4.2 \times 10^5 \text{ J}$ than its energy at 0 °C. According to Einstein's theory, that increase in energy has an increase in mass associated with it. The mass of the water will therefore be greater at 100 °C, because its energy is greater.

○ Use Einstein's equation to calculate the mass that is equivalent to $4.2 \times 10^5 \text{ J}$.

○ Einstein's equation can be rearranged to make m the subject by dividing both sides by c^2, and this gives $m = \dfrac{E}{c^2}$. So:

$$m = \frac{E}{c^2} = \frac{4.2 \times 10^5 \text{ J}}{(3.0 \times 10^8 \text{ m s}^{-1})^2} = 4.7 \times 10^{-12} \text{ kg}$$

This is an incredibly small mass. Not surprisingly, we are not aware of the change in the mass of the water when it is heated, and the mass changes associated with most other energy changes are undetectably small. The exception arises in nuclear reactions like those that occur in the Sun, and in nuclear power stations and nuclear weapons explosions, in which one element is converted into another. In these reactions, a significant proportion of the mass of the original element is converted into other forms of energy. The following question allows you to investigate this mass–energy conversion in the Sun.

Question 8.4   (a) When hydrogen is converted into helium in the core of the Sun, about 0.7% of the mass of hydrogen is converted into other forms of energy. How much energy is produced from 1 kg of hydrogen?

(b) The power output from the Sun is 4×10^{26} W. What mass of hydrogen must be converted into helium *each second* to produce this power?

(c) The Sun's mass is 2×10^{30} kg, and initially 75% of this was hydrogen (and most of the rest was helium). The rate at which hydrogen is converted into helium remains constant throughout the Sun's life, and it will reach the end of its life in the form we know it when the hydrogen in the hot central core — 15% of the hydrogen initially present in the Sun — has been converted into helium. Use this information to calculate the Sun's lifetime. ◀

The mass of hydrogen converted each second, which you calculated in the previous question, may seem inconceivably large. However, if you compare it with the mass of the Sun, which is 2×10^{30} kg, then it is very small, and this is why the Sun has a very long lifetime. As we pointed out in Block 3, astrophysicists estimate that the Sun has been shining for about five billion years, and has enough hydrogen left in the hot core to continue shining for about another five billion years. This adds up to 10 billion years between birth and death, which is the value calculated in Question 8.4. We will return to this topic in Block 11, after we have explored the world of atoms and nuclei and quarks in the next two blocks of the course.

8.4   Summary of Section 8

Electromagnetic radiation from the Sun is the ultimate source of energy for life on Earth.

Solar energy can be exploited indirectly through food and fuels whose stored energy derives mainly from solar energy, or through renewable resources such as hydroelectricity and wind. It can also be exploited directly using solar collectors and solar cells.

If the Earth had no atmosphere, its GMST would stabilize at a temperature of about −6 °C. In this steady state the rate at which longwave infrared radiation is emitted just balances the rate at which the incoming solar radiation is absorbed.

Mass is a form of energy. The energy associated with mass m is given by Einstein's equation $E = mc^2$. If the energy of an object increases, then its mass also increases.

The energy source within the Sun is the direct conversion of matter into other forms of energy as part of a nuclear fusion process in which hydrogen is converted into helium.

Energy — an overview

The concept of energy was first developed in the early 19th century, and initially it was confined to various forms of 'mechanical' energy — kinetic energy, gravitational energy and strain energy. It was James Joule who demonstrated in the mid-1800s that heat is a form of energy transfer, and that conversion of mechanical energy could produce a heating effect. Since then, the list of energy types has grown, but always within the framework of the law of conservation of energy. This law is firmly grounded in experimental measurements, and is one of the cornerstones of science. Indeed, if the known types of energy are not adequate to balance the observed energy inputs and outputs of a process, then a new form of energy transfer or conversion is postulated to account for the difference. Of course, every new form of energy (such as the energy associated with mass, which was unknown before Einstein came on the scene) must be defined in a way that is consistent with other forms of energy, and so far, all proposed new forms of energy have met this condition. This is why scientists have such faith in the concept of energy, and why conservation of energy provides a consistent framework for our understanding of the Universe.

We have discussed a variety of forms of energy in this block, and there are other forms that we have only mentioned briefly in passing, such as the energy associated with electromagnetic radiation, sound and earthquakes. At first sight the different forms of energy may seem rather disparate and unrelated. They are each defined by their own individual equation (and you may have found it difficult to remember the various equations involved), but as we have emphasized they are all linked by the law of conservation of energy. One form of energy can be converted into another, and when this happens, the books must always balance — the total amount of energy is always conserved.

As you study later blocks of this course, you will discover many new examples of the important roles that energy plays in the world of science. We will have a lot more to say about the energy associated with chemical reactions (Block 8), about the energy required for the metabolic reactions that are essential for life (Block 9), and about the energy of the natural environment (wind, rivers, etc.) that is responsible for transporting sedimentary materials from place to place (Block 10). You will meet energy on a very small scale — the tiny but very precisely defined amounts of energy associated with single atoms (Block 7) — and energy on a huge scale — the total amount of energy associated with the Universe at the moment of the Big Bang (Block 11). All of these examples will build on basic concepts about energy that have been presented in this block, and the most important of these is that energy is always conserved.

Activity 9.1   Reviewing your study of Block 5

In this final activity you will reflect on how well you are coping with new mathematics and with problem solving. ◄

Questions: answers and comments

In these answers, we always show the intermediate steps that are taken to reach the final result of each calculation, and we explain many of the steps. When doing the questions for yourself, we suggest that you set out your answers in a similar way, though your words of explanation may be briefer. This will be useful practice for assignments. SGSG Chapter 4 Section 5 (Expressing yourself mathematically) contains useful advice on setting out answers to calculations, and we recommend that you spend 15 minutes reading this, either now or when you have answered a few of the questions. Also, when you have completed a calculation, you should make sure that you have included appropriate units in the answer, and have quoted the appropriate number of significant figures, before checking your answer against ours.

Comments on the answers are given in curly brackets {…}.

Question 3.1   Using Equation 3.6, $W = Fd$, and substituting $F = 415$ N and $d = 15$ m, we get

$$W = Fd$$
$$= 415\,\text{N} \times 15\,\text{m}$$
$$= 6.225 \times 10^3\,\text{N m}$$
$$= 6.2 \times 10^3\,\text{N m (to two sig figs)}$$

But $1\,\text{N m} = 1\,\text{J}$ (Equation 3.7), so the work done on the car is

$$W = 6.2 \times 10^3\,\text{J}$$

{Note that we quote the answer to only two significant figures because the distance was only quoted to that level of precision (Block 2, Box 2.1).}

Question 3.2   Neither wrestler moves in the direction of the force which he is experiencing, so $d = 0$. Therefore as $W = Fd$, the work is equal to zero, and so no work is being done on either wrestler. {Note that this does *not* mean that no energy conversion is taking place — as both wrestlers would be at pains to point out. Chemical reactions take place in muscles to keep them in a state of contraction, and these reactions will release stored chemical energy, and the wrestlers will get rather warm!}

Question 3.3   To find the equation for the acceleration a, we need to cancel out the m on the right-hand side of the equation $F = ma$. We therefore divide both sides of

the equation by m:

$$F = ma$$

$$\frac{F}{m} = \frac{ma}{m} = a$$

where the ms cancel from the expression in the middle. Thus:

$$a = \frac{F}{m}$$

The acceleration is the force divided by the mass.

Question 3.4   We need to separate v from both u and t in $a = \dfrac{v - u}{t}$. First, we remove t from the right-hand side of the equation by multiplying both sides of the equation by t:

$$a = \frac{v - u}{t}$$

$$a \times t = \frac{v - u}{t} \times t \qquad \text{so} \qquad at = v - u$$

{As you learned in Block 1, multiplications and divisions have precedence over additions and subtractions (the BODMAS rule). So we multiply both sides by t to cancel out the ts, *before* adding u to both sides to cancel out the $-u$.}

To make v the subject, we add u to both sides:

$$at + u = v - u + u$$

The $-u$ and the $+u$ on the right cancel, so we are left with

$$at + u = v \qquad \text{or} \qquad v = at + u$$

Question 3.5   {Although this equation may look more complicated than ones you have met so far, it is just as easy to manipulate because the d^2 term can be treated as a single term.}

To make I the subject of the equation $v = \dfrac{kI}{d^2}$, we first multiply both sides by d^2 (to cancel the d^2 on the right of the equation):

$$v = \frac{kI}{d^2}$$

$$d^2 \times v = d^2 \times \frac{kI}{d^2}$$

$$d^2 v = kI$$

and we then divide both sides by k (to cancel the k on the right):

$$\frac{d^2 v}{k} = \frac{kI}{k}, \qquad \frac{d^2 v}{k} = I, \qquad \text{so} \qquad I = \frac{d^2 v}{k}$$

Question 3.6   We need to calculate d, so we rearrange the equation $W = Fd$ (Equation 3.6) to make d the subject by dividing both sides by F and swapping the left and right-hand sides.

$$d = \frac{W}{F}$$

We then substitute the following values, $W = 2.8 \times 10^2\,$J and $F = 2.79 \times 10^4\,$N, to find:

$$d = \frac{2.8 \times 10^2\,\text{J}}{2.79 \times 10^4\,\text{N}} = 0.010\,\text{J N}^{-1} \text{ (to two sig figs)}$$

But $1\,\text{J} = 1\,\text{N} \times 1\,\text{m}$, so $1\,\text{J N}^{-1} = 1\,\text{N} \times 1\,\text{m} \times \text{N}^{-1} = 1\,\text{m}$, and therefore:

$$d = 0.010\,\text{m, or } 1.0\,\text{cm}$$

{Note the relatively small amount of work involved in lifting this enormous mass through a small distance. Note also that you did not need to use the value of the mass quoted in the question, since the value of the force was given.}

Question 3.7   Since $a = 4zr$ (second equation), we can eliminate the a from the first equation by substituting $4zr$ in place of it:

$$x = \frac{2z^2}{a} = \frac{2z^2}{4zr}$$

Now $z^2 = z \times z$, and one of these z terms will cancel the z on the bottom of the fraction:

$$x = \frac{2z \times z}{4zr} \qquad \text{so} \qquad x = \frac{z}{2r}$$

Question 3.8   Since $t = 2z$, we can eliminate t from the first equation by substituting $2z$:

$$y = 3t^2 + v = 3(2z)^2 + v$$

{Don't forget to include the brackets as $(2z)^2$ is not the same as $2z^2$.}

Now $(2z)^2 = 2z \times 2z = 4z^2$, so

$$y = 3 \times 4z^2 + v$$

Thus $\qquad y = 12z^2 + v$

Question 3.9   (a) $3.2^2 = 10.24$; $17.4^2 = 302.76$; $8.3^2 = 68.89$; $0.5^2 = 0.25$. Expressing these answers to the same number of significant figures as in the question, we get 10; 303; 69; 0.3.

(b) $\sqrt{80} = 8.9$; $\sqrt{111} = 10.5$; $\sqrt{1015.3} = 31.864$; $\sqrt{0.5} = 0.7$.

(c) To get t^2 on its own, we multiply both sides of the equation $d = \frac{1}{2}at^2$ by 2 and divide both sides by a:

$$d \times \frac{2}{a} = \frac{1}{2}at^2 \times \frac{2}{a}$$

Since the 2s and the as cancel on the right of the equation, we obtain:

$$\frac{2d}{a} = t^2 \qquad \text{or} \qquad t^2 = \frac{2d}{a}$$

Taking the square roots of both sides of the equation, we get:

$$\sqrt{t^2} = \sqrt{\frac{2d}{a}} \qquad \text{so} \qquad t = \sqrt{\frac{2d}{a}}$$

{Note that the square root sign stretches across both top and bottom of the fraction, and this means 'the square root of $\frac{2d}{a}$'. If we wrote $\frac{\sqrt{2d}}{a}$ this would mean something quite different, namely 'the square root of $2d$, divided by a'.}

Question 3.10   The train is frictionless, so since energy is conserved the work done must equal the change in kinetic energy. The train's mass m is $200\,$g $= 0.200\,$kg, its initial speed u is $1.0\,$m s^{-1}, and its final speed v is $2.0\,$m s^{-1}. So, the initial kinetic energy is:

$$E_k = \frac{1}{2}mu^2$$
$$= \frac{1}{2} \times 0.200\,\text{kg} \times (1.0\,\text{m s}^{-1})^2 = 0.10\,\text{J}$$

and the final kinetic energy is:

$$E_k = \frac{1}{2}mv^2$$
$$= \frac{1}{2} \times 0.200\,\text{kg} \times (2.0\,\text{m s}^{-1})^2 = 0.40\,\text{J}$$

So the change in kinetic energy is $(0.40 - 0.10)$ J, which is 0.30 J to two significant figures. As the change in kinetic energy is equal to the work done on the train, it follows that the work done is also 0.30 J.

Question 3.11 If there is friction within the train mechanism, then there will be a continual conversion of kinetic energy into internal energy. This means that the kinetic energy of the train will decrease steadily until it is zero, and so the speed of the train will decrease steadily, and the train will eventually stop.

Question 3.12 The energy transferred to the car in 30 s is 6.2×10^3 J. The power is calculated from Equation 3.17 as:

$$P = \frac{E}{t} = \frac{6.2 \times 10^3 \text{ J}}{30 \text{ s}}$$

$$= 2.067 \times 10^2 \text{ J s}^{-1}$$

$$= 2.1 \times 10^2 \text{ J s}^{-1} \text{ (to two sig figs)}$$

$$= 2.1 \times 10^2 \text{ W, or } 210 \text{ W}$$

Question 3.13 In order to calculate the length of time the club and ball were in contact, we rearrange Equation 3.17 to make t the subject (by multiplying both sides by t and dividing both by P):

$$t = \frac{E}{P}$$

The initial speed of the golf ball is zero, so the energy transferred to the ball, E, is equal to the ball's final kinetic energy:

$$E = E_k = \tfrac{1}{2} mv^2$$

$$= \tfrac{1}{2} \times 5.0 \times 10^{-2} \text{ kg} \times (80 \text{ m s}^{-1})^2 = 160 \text{ J}$$

Also $P = 3.1$ kW $= 3.1 \times 10^3$ W. So

$$t = \frac{160 \text{ J}}{3.1 \times 10^3 \text{ W}} = 5.161 \times 10^{-2} \frac{\text{J}}{\text{J s}^{-1}}$$

$$= 5.2 \times 10^{-2} \text{ s (to two sig figs)}$$

{Note that we used the relationship $1 \text{ W} = 1 \text{ J s}^{-1}$ to work out the units of the answer.}

Have you been comparing the way that you set out your answers to calculations with the versions printed here? You may wish to read again the advice at the beginning of this answers section on p. 58 and refer to the section of *SGSG* mentioned there.

Question 4.1 We know that when any object near the Earth's surface is acted on by the gravitational force alone, it has acceleration $g = 9.8$ m s^{-2}. So applying Newton's second law of motion, the gravitational force is

$$F_g = ma = mg$$

(a) For a person with $m = 80$ kg:

$$F_g = 80 \text{ kg} \times 9.8 \text{ m s}^{-2} = 784 \text{ kg m s}^{-2}$$

$$= 780 \text{ N (to two sig figs)}$$

(b) For a 100 g bar of chocolate, we substitute $m = 0.10$ kg into the equation $F_g = mg$, and in this case the gravitational force is 0.98 N, which is about 1 N. {So if you want to know what 1 N feels like, pick up a 100 g object and experience the force that it exerts on your hand.}

Question 4.2 (a) A person with mass m has weight mg. On Earth, $g = 9.8$ m s^{-2}, so the weight of an 80 kg person is $80 \text{ kg} \times 9.8 \text{ m s}^{-2} = 780$ N (to two sig figs). {This is the same as the value you calculated in Question 4.1, since the weight of an object is the same as the gravitational force that acts on it. Next time you are asked your weight, you might like to give the value in newtons — and then explain to your friends the difference between the scientific and everyday use of the term weight!}

(b) On the Moon, $g = 1.6$ m s^{-2}, so in this case

$$\text{weight} = 80 \text{ kg} \times 1.6 \text{ m s}^{-2} = 130 \text{ N (to two sig figs)}$$

{This shows that the weight of an object on the Moon is roughly one-sixth of its weight on Earth, even though its mass is the same in both places.}

Question 4.3 (a) The work done by gravity is $W = mgh$. You were asked to *estimate* the work done, so you need to estimate values for the mass of this book and for the height of your table. My estimates were $m = 0.1$ kg and $h = 0.8$ m. With these values, and using a value for g of 10 m s^{-2}, the work done on the book by gravity as it falls is:

$$W = mgh = 0.1 \text{ kg} \times 10 \text{ m s}^{-2} \times 0.8 \text{ m}$$

$$= 0.8 \text{ J (to one sig fig)}$$

{Your estimated values may have been somewhat different, but your answer shouldn't differ from mine by more than a factor of two. If it does, think again about your estimated values.}

(b) The kinetic energy just before impact will be equal to the work done, so it is 0.8 J too. We can work out the speed from this kinetic energy by using Equation 3.14,

$$v = \sqrt{\frac{2E_k}{m}}$$

and substituting $E_k = 0.8$ J and $m = 0.1$ kg. So

$$v = \sqrt{\frac{2 \times 0.8\,\mathrm{J}}{0.1\,\mathrm{kg}}} = \sqrt{16\,\mathrm{J\,kg^{-1}}}$$

$$= 4\,\mathrm{m\,s^{-1}} \text{ (to one sig fig)}$$

{The SI unit of speed is $\mathrm{m\,s^{-1}}$, and we can show that this is equivalent to $\sqrt{\mathrm{J\,kg^{-1}}}$ as follows:

$$1\,\mathrm{J} = 1\,\mathrm{kg\,m^2\,s^{-2}}$$

so $1\,\mathrm{J\,kg^{-1}} = 1\,\mathrm{kg\,m^2\,s^{-2}\,kg^{-1}} = 1\,\mathrm{m^2\,s^{-2}}$

and so $\sqrt{\mathrm{J\,kg^{-1}}} = \sqrt{1\,\mathrm{m^2\,s^{-2}}} = 1\,\mathrm{m\,s^{-1}}$}

(c) The kinetic energy will be zero after the book comes to rest on the floor. However, energy is always conserved, so the kinetic energy must be converted into other forms of energy, in particular, to sound energy and internal energy of the book and the floor.

{Sound is transmitted as a pressure wave — just like the seismic P waves that you saw animated in CD-ROM Activity 10.2 in Block 3. As sound waves spread out, the molecules in the air collide with each other and with molecules of objects that they strike, and the energy transported by the sound wave is eventually converted into internal energy.}

Question 4.4 (a) In this question we have to calculate the initial speed of the arrow, and all we are told is the height, 25 m, that it must reach. The arrow will just reach the damsel if the maximum height it reaches is 25 m, and at this point the arrow will have zero speed for an instant, and zero kinetic energy. So all of its initial kinetic energy has been converted into gravitational energy when it reaches this point, assuming there is no air resistance. The initial kinetic energy is $E_k = \frac{1}{2} mu^2$, where u is the initial speed, and the increase in gravitational energy is $\Delta E_g = mg\Delta h$, where Δh is the maximum height. Since energy is conserved we can equate these two terms:

$$mg\Delta h = \tfrac{1}{2} mu^2$$

We want to calculate the value of u, so we need to make u the subject of this equation. We first multiply both sides by 2 and divided both by m:

$$mg\Delta h \times \frac{2}{m} = \frac{1}{2} mu^2 \times \frac{2}{m}$$

$$u^2 = 2g\Delta h$$

and then take the square root of both sides:

$$u = \sqrt{2g\Delta h}$$

If the values of g and Δh are substituted into the equation, we find:

$$u = \sqrt{2 \times 9.8\,\mathrm{m\,s^{-2}} \times 25\,\mathrm{m}} = \sqrt{490\,\mathrm{m^2\,s^{-2}}}$$

$$= 22\,\mathrm{m\,s^{-1}} \text{ (to two sig figs)}$$

(b) As the arrow falls, the stored gravitational energy will be converted back into kinetic energy, and if it falls 25 m then its kinetic energy will be the same as that with which it started. The arrow's speed will therefore be the same as the speed with which it was released, that is $22\,\mathrm{m\,s^{-1}}$.

Question 4.5 We need to calculate the final speed of the skier, and we are given the initial and final altitudes, and the initial speed. If we assume friction and air resistance are negligible, the sum of the skier's kinetic energy and gravitational energy must remain constant throughout the run. So the gravitational energy that she loses as she descends is all converted into kinetic energy. The loss of gravitational energy is $\Delta E_g = mg\Delta h$, where Δh is the 100 m difference between the initial and final altitudes. The increase in kinetic energy is the difference between the kinetic energy at the finish $\frac{1}{2} mv^2$ and the kinetic energy at the start $\frac{1}{2} mu^2$. So:

$$mg\Delta h = \tfrac{1}{2} mv^2 - \tfrac{1}{2} mu^2$$

{Note that the skier's speed is increasing, so v is greater than u, and the increase in kinetic energy must be $\frac{1}{2} mv^2 - \frac{1}{2} mu^2$, which has a positive value, rather than $\frac{1}{2} mu^2 - \frac{1}{2} mv^2$.} We want to know the final speed v, so the equation needs some rearrangement. We first divide both sides by m, and this means that on the right we have to divide both $\frac{1}{2} mv^2$ and $\frac{1}{2} mu^2$ by m; this cancels all of the ms in the equation:

$$g\Delta h = \tfrac{1}{2} v^2 - \tfrac{1}{2} u^2$$

Then multiply both sides by 2:

$$2g\Delta h = v^2 - u^2$$

and add u^2 to both sides, so that v^2 is left on its own on the right:

$$2g\Delta h + u^2 = v^2$$

We can now interchange the two sides of the equation and substitute the values given in the question:

$$v^2 = 2g\Delta h + u^2 = (2 \times 9.8\,\text{m}\,\text{s}^{-2} \times 100\,\text{m}) + (10\,\text{m}\,\text{s}^{-1})^2$$
$$= 1\,960\,\text{m}^2\,\text{s}^{-2} + 100\,\text{m}^2\,\text{s}^{-2} = 2\,060\,\text{m}^2\,\text{s}^{-2}$$

{In substituting the values at this point in the calculation, you may feel we have not followed the good practice set out in Box 4.2. However, in cases such as this, it is often easier to work out v^2 to save having to deal with several terms under a square root sign.}

Finally, we take the square root of both sides to get the value of v:

$$v = \sqrt{2\,060\,\text{m}^2\,\text{s}^{-2}} = 45\,\text{m}\,\text{s}^{-1} \text{ (to two sig figs)}$$

{This is approximately 100 miles per hour! In reality, the final speed would be much less due to the combined effects of friction between the skis and snow, and air resistance. Notice that you didn't have to consider the complexities of the ski path to answer this question. Because of the law of conservation of energy, all you needed to know were the initial and final heights, or, to be more specific, the difference between the initial and final heights.}

Question 4.6 (a) The change in gravitational energy is calculated from $\Delta E_g = mg\Delta h$ (Equation 4.8), so substituting the values of mass ($m = 80\,\text{kg}$) and height difference ($\Delta h = 5.5\,\text{cm} = 0.055\,\text{m}$) quoted in the question, we find:

$$\Delta E_g = 80\,\text{kg} \times 9.8\,\text{m}\,\text{s}^{-2} \times 0.055\,\text{m} = 43\,\text{J} \text{ (to two sig figs)}$$

(b) The speed of the bob is zero at the highest point of the swing, so its kinetic energy is zero there too. As the bob swings down, gravitational energy is converted into kinetic energy, and the kinetic energy will be greatest at the lowest point, where the gravitational energy has its lowest value. This will therefore be the point where the speed has its maximum value.

Assuming that air resistance is negligible, conservation of energy tells us that the maximum kinetic energy of the pendulum is equal to the decrease in its gravitational energy. So:

$$E_k = \tfrac{1}{2}mv^2 = \Delta E_g$$

If we multiply both sides by 2 and divide by m, we get:

$$v^2 = \frac{2\Delta E_g}{m}$$

{Once again, it is easier to substitute the values into the equation before finding the square root.} As $\Delta E_g = 43\,\text{J}$ and $m = 80\,\text{kg}$:

$$v^2 = \frac{2 \times 43\,\text{J}}{80\,\text{kg}} = 1.075\,\text{m}^2\,\text{s}^{-2}$$

If we take the square root of this value:

$$v = 1.0\,\text{m}\,\text{s}^{-1} \text{ (to two sig figs)}$$

{Note that the information about the length of the cable and the distance through which the bob swings was not needed to answer this question, but was included for interest, and to give you practice in selecting the information needed to answer questions.}

Question 5.1 We assume that the chemical energy from the 5 g of ice cream is converted via Mrs Jones' internal organs and muscles into the gravitational energy she acquires as she climbs the stairs.

We are told in the text that 100 g of ice cream provides $1.05 \times 10^6\,\text{J}$, so 5 g provides:

$$\frac{5}{100} \times 1.05 \times 10^6\,\text{J} = 5 \times 10^4\,\text{J} \text{ (to one sig fig)}$$

To get back to her flat Mrs Jones has to climb 52 steps, each 0.18 m high, so:

$$\Delta h = 52 \times 0.18\,\text{m} = 9.36\,\text{m}$$

So her gravitational energy increases by:

$$\Delta E_g = mg\Delta h = 60\,\text{kg} \times 9.8\,\text{m}\,\text{s}^{-2} \times 9.36\,\text{m} = 5.5 \times 10^3\,\text{J}$$

The energy available from 5 g of ice cream is about ten times greater than the gravitational energy she gains when she returns to her flat. {Of course, some chemical energy will be converted into internal energy in Mrs Jones' body as she climbs the stairs, so she will actually convert more than the $5.5 \times 10^3\,\text{J}$ required to increase her gravitational energy. However, the large difference between the two numbers indicates that a lot of exercise is needed to compensate for extra food intake!}

Question 6.1 (a) We can calculate the energy required to heat the copper pan by using Equation 6.3, $q = cm\Delta T$, and substituting the values $c = 3.8 \times 10^2 \, J \, kg^{-1} \, °C^{-1}$ (from Table 6.1), $m = 0.50 \, kg$, and $\Delta T = 80 \, °C$:

$$q = (3.8 \times 10^2 \, J \, kg^{-1} \, °C^{-1}) \times (0.50 \, kg) \times (80 \, °C)$$
$$= 1.52 \times 10^4 \, J$$

(b) (i) A 250 g (0.25 kg) copper pan has half the mass of the 0.50 kg pan in part (a). Since the energy required is proportional to the mass, this smaller pan will require half of the energy that you calculated as the answer to part (a), i.e. $7.6 \times 10^3 \, J$.

(ii) The energy required is also proportional to the specific heat of the material from which the pan is made. The specific heat of aluminium is greater than that of copper, so the energy required to heat it will be greater. Since we only asked for an 'estimate' we can say that the specific heat of aluminium is about twice that of copper, so the energy required will be about double the value calculated in part (a), i.e. $2 \times 1.52 \times 10^4 \, J = 3 \times 10^4 \, J$. {This estimate is made for copper and aluminium pans that have the same *mass*. In practice, because aluminium has a much lower density that copper, the energy required for pans with *similar dimensions* is about the same. However, copper pans conduct heat better than aluminium, so many cooks prefer them for this reason.}

Question 6.2 (a) To convert temperature in degrees Celsius into temperature in kelvin, you have to add 273.15 to the value of the Celsius temperature, so:

$$\left(\begin{array}{c} \text{temperature} \\ \text{in kelvin} \end{array}\right) = \left(\begin{array}{c} \text{temperature in} \\ \text{degrees Celsius} \end{array}\right) + 273.15$$

(b) If you then rearrange the equation in part (a) to make temperature in degrees Celsius the subject of the equation (by subtracting 273.15 from both sides) you get:

$$\left(\begin{array}{c} \text{temperature in} \\ \text{degrees Celsius} \end{array}\right) = \left(\begin{array}{c} \text{temperature} \\ \text{in kelvin} \end{array}\right) - 273.15$$

Question 6.3 Since the poker was initially at a much higher temperature than the ale, the metal atoms had a much greater mean kinetic energy than the water molecules. So when water molecules collided with the hot poker, they generally gained energy at the expense of the metal atoms. Many of the water molecules gained sufficient energy to escape from the ale as water vapour. As the metal atoms lost energy to the colliding water molecules, they vibrated less vigorously, which meant that the temperature of the poker fell. Eventually the ale

and the poker reached the same temperature, and then the mean kinetic energy of the metal atoms and the water molecules were the same. There was then no net transfer of energy between the metal atoms and the water molecules. {To simplify the answer, we have ignored the alcohol molecules in the ale. However, if you read the answer again, but substitute 'alcohol' for 'water', then it correctly describes what happened to the alcohol molecules.}

Question 6.4 (a) To find the temperature in kelvin, you add 273.15 to the temperature in degrees Celsius. So the boiling temperature of liquid oxygen is $(-183 + 273.15) \, K = 90 \, K$. {Note that the answer is given to the nearest kelvin, because the Celsius temperature was given to the nearest °C. Remember, in Block 2, Box 2.2, we showed that when adding and subtracting quantities, the number of decimal places given in the answer should be the same as the smallest number of decimal places in the quantities involved in the calculation.}

(b) If we assume that all of the heat q transferred to the flask provides the latent heat to vaporize liquid oxygen, then $q = Lm$, where L is the value of the latent heat of vaporization for oxygen, $2.1 \times 10^5 \, J \, kg^{-1}$ (from Table 6.2), and m is the mass that is vaporized. If this equation is rearranged to make m the subject:

$$m = \frac{q}{L} = \frac{9.5 \times 10^4 \, J}{2.1 \times 10^5 \, J \, kg^{-1}} = 0.45 \, kg$$

Since the value of the heat transferred used in the calculation is the amount transferred in an hour, the mass of 0.45 kg is the mass vaporized in an hour.

Question 6.5 The energy q required to evaporate $5.1 \times 10^{17} \, kg$ of water, which has a latent heat of vaporization of $L = 2.6 \times 10^6 \, J \, kg^{-1}$, is given by Equation 6.6:

$$q = Lm = (2.6 \times 10^6 \, J \, kg^{-1}) \times (5.1 \times 10^{17} \, kg)$$
$$= 1.3 \times 10^{24} \, J \text{ (to two sig figs)}$$

Question 7.1 This is a rather personal calculation! My mass is 65 kg, so there are about 65×10^{26} electrons in my body, or 6.5×10^{27} using scientific notation. The total charge of all of the electrons will be the number of electrons multiplied by the charge on each electron, so:

$$\text{charge of electrons} = (6.5 \times 10^{27}) \times (-1.6 \times 10^{-19} \, C)$$

This is about $-1 \times 10^9 \, C$. As I am electrically neutral, there must also be a total positive charge of $+1 \times 10^9$ C in my body. {You will have a different mass, and therefore the charges that you have calculated will be different; however, they are unlikely to differ from the answers above by more than a factor of about two.}

Question 7.2 Atoms are electrically neutral overall because each atom has equal amounts of negative and positive charge. So, as you are made of atoms, your body as a whole is electrically neutral. As there is no electrical force between neutral objects, there can be no electrical force between you and another person in the same room.

Alternatively, you may argue that for two humans there will be *repulsive* forces (i) between their 10^9 C of negative charge, and (ii) between their 10^9 C of positive charge. But then you would have to argue that there will also be the same size *attractive* forces (i) between the 10^9 C of negative charge of one of them and the 10^9 C of positive charge of the other and also (ii) between the 10^9 C of positive charge of the first and the 10^9 C of negative charge of the second. The total repulsive force will exactly cancel out the total attractive force, so the two humans can sit together happily.

Question 7.3 The change in electrical energy is found using Equation 7.4:

$$\Delta E_e = Q\Delta V = 2\,C \times 12\,V = 24\,C\,V$$
$$= 24\,J \text{ (since } 1\,C\,V = 1\,J)$$

Question 7.4 Power is related to current and voltage difference by Equation 7.7, $P = I\Delta V$. In this case the current is 8.4 A and the voltage difference is 240 V, and so:

$$P = 8.4\,A \times 240\,V = 2\,016\,A\,V$$

Now $1\,A \times 1\,V = 1\,W$, so the power rating of the element is 2 016 W, or 2.0 kW to two significant figures.

Question 7.5 (a) We first rearrange Equation 7.7, $P = I\Delta V$, to make the current I the subject (by dividing both sides by ΔV), and the resulting equation is:

$$I = \frac{P}{\Delta V}$$

If we substitute the values for the power (20 W) and the voltage difference (12 V) into this equation, we get:

$$I = \frac{20\,W}{12\,V} = 1.67\,A, \text{ or } 1.7\,A \text{ (to two sig figs)}$$

(b) To find the charge that flows in one minute, we rearrange Equation 7.1, $I = \dfrac{Q}{t}$, to make Q the subject. The resulting equation is:

$$Q = It = 1.67\,A \times 60\,s = 100\,A\,s$$
$$= 100\,C \text{ (to two sig figs)}$$

Question 8.1 You may have thought of some of the following:

- wind power — wind is caused by uneven heating of the atmosphere by solar energy;

- water power — solar energy drives the water cycle, and electricity can be generated when water flows 'downhill' through water turbines in hydroelectric power stations;

- wave power — waves are generated by the wind, which in turn is generated by solar energy.

Question 8.2 The SI unit of power P is the W, for area A it is m^2, and for temperature T it is kelvin, K. You were told that the unit for σ is W m^{-2} K^{-4}, so

$$\text{unit of } (\sigma A T^4) = (\text{W m}^{-2}\,\text{K}^{-4}) \times \text{m}^2 \times \text{K}^4$$

The m^{-2} and the m^2 cancel each other out, and the K^{-4} and the K^4 also cancel, so the unit of $\sigma A T^4$ is simply W. This is the same as the unit of power P on the left of Equation 8.1. So the units on the two sides of the equation balance, as they must do.

Question 8.3 (a) 85% of the solar electromagnetic radiation reaching the Earth will be absorbed by the Earth's surface, so the rate at which energy is absorbed is:

$$P = 1.74 \times 10^{17}\,\text{W} \times \frac{85}{100} = 1.48 \times 10^{17}\,\text{W}$$

(b) In the steady state the Earth must be losing energy at the same rate at which it is gaining energy (remember the leaky tank!). If there were no atmosphere, the only way the Earth's surface would lose energy would be by emission of infrared radiation. So the rate of emission of infrared radiation in the steady state would be 1.48×10^{17} W, the same as the rate of absorption calculated in part (a).

(c) The power of the radiation emitted by the Earth's surface at $-6\,°$C is given by Equation 8.1, $P = \sigma A T^4$. The value of the constant σ is quoted below Equation 8.1 (5.67×10^{-8} W m^{-2} K^{-4}) and the area A of the Earth's surface is $5.1 \times 10^{14}\,\text{m}^2$. The temperature that we substitute must be in the SI unit kelvin (Section 6.3), so we must first convert $-6\,°C$ into kelvin:

$$T = (-6 + 273)\,\text{K} = 267\,\text{K}$$

We then substitute the values into Equation 8.1:

$$P = (5.67 \times 10^{-8}\,\text{W m}^{-2}\,\text{K}^{-4}) \times (5.1 \times 10^{14}\,\text{m}^2)$$
$$\times (267\,\text{K})^4$$
$$= 1.47 \times 10^{17}\,\text{W}$$

(where we have used the fact that $T^4 = T \times T \times T \times T$ to calculate the value of T^4). This value is just slightly smaller than the value that you calculated in part (b) for the rate at which infrared radiation would need to be emitted by the Earth's surface in the steady state with no atmosphere. This indicates that the Earth's GMST would be about $267\,\text{K}$, or $-6\,°C$, in the steady state with no atmosphere. {Of course, this is a rather unreal calculation, because removing the atmosphere would have other effects, such as changing the albedo of the Earth's surface as vegetation disappeared and ice cover increased.}

Question 8.4   (a) 0.7% of 1 kg of hydrogen is $\frac{0.7}{100} \times 1\,\text{kg}$ $= 7 \times 10^{-3}\,\text{kg}$. We use Einstein's equation, $E = mc^2$, to calculate how much energy this is equivalent to:

$$E = mc^2 = 7 \times 10^{-3}\,\text{kg} \times (3 \times 10^8\,\text{m s}^{-1})^2$$
$$= 6 \times 10^{14}\,\text{J (to one sig fig)}$$

(b) The Sun's power output is $4 \times 10^{26}\,\text{W}$, which is $4 \times 10^{26}\,\text{J s}^{-1}$. Now from part (a) we know that

$$6 \times 10^{14}\,\text{J is released from 1 kg hydrogen,}$$

so   1 J is released from $\dfrac{1}{6 \times 10^{14}}\,\text{kg}$

and $4 \times 10^{26}\,\text{J}$ is released from $\dfrac{1 \times 4 \times 10^{26}}{6 \times 10^{14}}\,\text{kg}$

which is $7 \times 10^{11}\,\text{kg}$. This is the mass of hydrogen that is converted into helium *each second*, since we used the energy released each second ($4 \times 10^{26}\,\text{J}$) in this calculation.

(c) The time t required to convert all of the hydrogen into helium is given by:

$$t = \frac{\left(\begin{array}{c}\text{mass of hydrogen converted}\\ \text{during lifetime of Sun}\end{array}\right)}{\left(\begin{array}{c}\text{mass of hydrogen}\\ \text{converted per second}\end{array}\right)}$$

Now 75% of the initial mass of the Sun was hydrogen, i.e. $\frac{75}{100} \times 2 \times 10^{30}\,\text{kg} = 1.5 \times 10^{30}\,\text{kg}$, and 15% of this will be converted into helium during the Sun's lifetime, which is $\frac{15}{100} \times 1.5 \times 10^{30}\,\text{kg} = 2 \times 10^{29}\,\text{kg}$. So

$$t = \frac{2 \times 10^{29}\,\text{kg}}{7 \times 10^{11}\,\text{kg s}^{-1}} = 3 \times 10^{17}\,\text{s}$$

The number of seconds in a year is $365 \times 24 \times 60 \times 60 = 3.2 \times 10^7$, so the Sun's lifetime is:

$$t = \frac{3 \times 10^{17}}{3.2 \times 10^7}\,\text{y} = 1 \times 10^{10}\,\text{y, or 10 billion years}$$

Acknowledgements

Grateful acknowledgement is made to the following sources for permission to reproduce material in this block:

Figures

Figure 2.3: Palomar Observatory, California Institute of Technology. Image courtesy of the Smithsonian Institute, Washington; *Figure 3.4*: Colorsport; *Figure 6.2*: courtesy of Trond Erik Hillestad; *Figure 8.1*: ETSU/Department of Trade and Industry; *Figure 8.3*: Science Photo Library/NASA.

Title page photographs

Sunset: Science Photo Library/Pekka Parvainen; *Nuclear Power Station*: Science Photo Library/Martin Bond.

Index

Entries and page numbers in **bold type** refer to key words which are printed in **bold** in the text and which are defined in the Glossary. These are terms that we expect you to be able to explain the meaning of, and use correctly, both during and at the end of the course. An entry followed by ^{G} indicates a term which is defined in the Glossary but which is not bold in the text. Where the page number is given in *italics*, the indexed information is carried mainly or wholly in an illustration or table. Section summaries and answers to questions are not indexed.

absolute temperature scale 40–**41**
absolute zero 41
acceleration 17–18
    of falling object 25–6
    unit 19
acceleration due to gravity 26
air resistance^G 37, 38
algebra^G 5, 9, 16–18
    manipulating, in problems 30–1
    see also equations
ampere (unit) **49**
atmosphere 38, 43, 53–4
atoms 36–7, 46, 47
attractive force
    between molecules 36
    between unlike charges 46

battery, electric 48, 49–50
Boxes
    3.1 more about proportionality 11–12
    3.2 rearranging and solving equations 14–15
    3.3 combining algebraic equations 16
    3.4 getting the correct units 19–20
    3.5 squares and square roots 20–1
    4.1 estimating 27
    4.2 manipulating algebra in problems 30–1

calculator, use of
    for square roots 21
    for squares 20
change of state 37, 41–4
charge, electric 45–6, 48–9
    unit 46
chemical energy 6, 34, **37**
chemical reactions 37
conductor, electrical 47, 48
conservation of energy *see* law of conservation of energy
constant of proportionality 11–**12**, 25, 40, 42
coulomb (unit) **46**
current, electric 48–9, 51

delta (Δ) **22**

Earth
    evaporation from surface 43–4
    surface temperature *see* global mean surface temperature

Einstein's equation 54–5
electric battery 48, 49–50
electric charge 45–**46**, 48–9
    unit 46
electric current 48–9, 51
electric force 46
electric power 50–1
electrical conductor^G 47, 48
electrical energy 6, 45–**50**
electrical insulator^G 47
electrons 46–7, 48
energy^G 57
    in biological systems 34–5
    forms of 6–7, 45
    stored 32, 34
    from Sun *see* solar energy
    unit 12–13, 19
energy conservation
    and gravitational energy 29–32
    in locust's jump 35, 37
    see also law of conservation of energy
energy conversion 5, 6–7, 34, 35, 37, 38
    rate *see* power
    in resting individual 34
energy–mass equivalence 54–5
energy transfer 5, 6–7
    see also heat, work
equations 9, 12, 24, 44
    combining 16
    rearranging and solving 14–15, 21, 30–1
    symbols in 9
estimating^G 27

falling objects 25–6, 27
food, energy content 34
force
    electric 46
    gravitational 25–6
    unit 19
    work done by 10–11, 12–13
friction^G 22–3, 38

global mean surface temperature 41, 43, 53–4
gravitational energy 6, **28**–9, 36
    and energy conservation 29–32, 35
gravitational force^G 25, 26, 27
gravity^G
    acceleration due to 26
    motion under 25–32

work done against 27–9
work done by 26–7

heat 38–**39**, 40
    transfer 39
Hubble Space Telescope 53

insulator, electrical 47
internal energy 6, 7, 34, 36–**37**
    increasing by heating 38–9
    kinetic energy conversion to 37–8
ion 47, 48
joule (unit) 13, 14, 19

kelvin (unit) **41**
kelvin scale *see* absolute temperature scale
kinetic energy 6, **18**, 22, 28, 31
    conversion to gravitational energy 31–2, 35
    conversion to internal energy 37–8
    equation for 18
    of molecules 36, 37

latent heat of vaporization 41–**42**
    and Earth's surface temperature 43–4
    measuring 42
law of conservation of energy 5, **7**, 22, 28, 29, 31, 57
locust, jumping 35, 37

mass^G
    and gravitational force 25–6
    and Newton's second law 17
    and weight 26
    unit 19
mass–energy equivalence 54–5
meteor 38
molecules 36–37
    and air resistance 37–8
    and heat transfer 38–9
    and internal energy 36–7

newton (unit) 13
Newton's first law of motion 10
Newton's second law of motion 17, 25, 26
nuclear fusion^G, in Sun 2, 54–6
nuclear power station 2

particle model of matter 36–7
pendulum 32

photosynthesis 52
potential energy 32
    forms of 32–3
    gravitational *see* gravitational energy
    of molecules 36–7
    strain 32
powerG 23
    electric 50–1
    of emitted radiation 53
    nuclear *2*
    output from Sun 55
    from solar panels *53*
practical work 40
problem solving 20, 21, 30
proportionalityG 10, 11
    constant of 11–12, 25, 40, 42

quantum theory 7n.

repulsive force 46
respiration 52

semiconductors 47
solar cell 53
solar collector 52–3
solar energy 52–6
    and Earth's GMST 53–4
    electromagnetic radiation 44, 53
    source *2*, 54, 55
    uses 52–3
solving equationsG 14–15, 16, 30–1
    problems 20, 21, 30
sound energy 6
specific heat 39–40
    measuring for water 40
springs, strain energy in 32
square root 20–1
square 20
strain energy 32
study, reviewing 9, 57
substitutingG in equations 16, 19, 30
Sun, energy from *see* solar energy
swing 31–2
symbols, in algebraic equations 9, 24, 44

temperature
    absolute scale 40–1
    effect of heat transfer 39
    and internal energy 36, 38–9

units 19–20
    acceleration 19
    electric charge 46
    electric current 49
    energy 12–13, 14, 19
    equivalent 19
    force 19
    latent heat of vaporization 42
    mass 19
    power 23
    specific heat 40
    temperature 41
    voltage difference 50
    work 12–13, 14

volt (unit) **50**
voltage difference (voltage) **50**

water
    measuring latent heat of vaporization 42
    measuring specific heat 40
water cycle 43–4
watt (unit) 23
weight 26, 27
work 9, **10**–11, 12–13
    calculating 13–14
    done against gravity 27–9
    done by gravity 26–7
    unit 12–13, 14